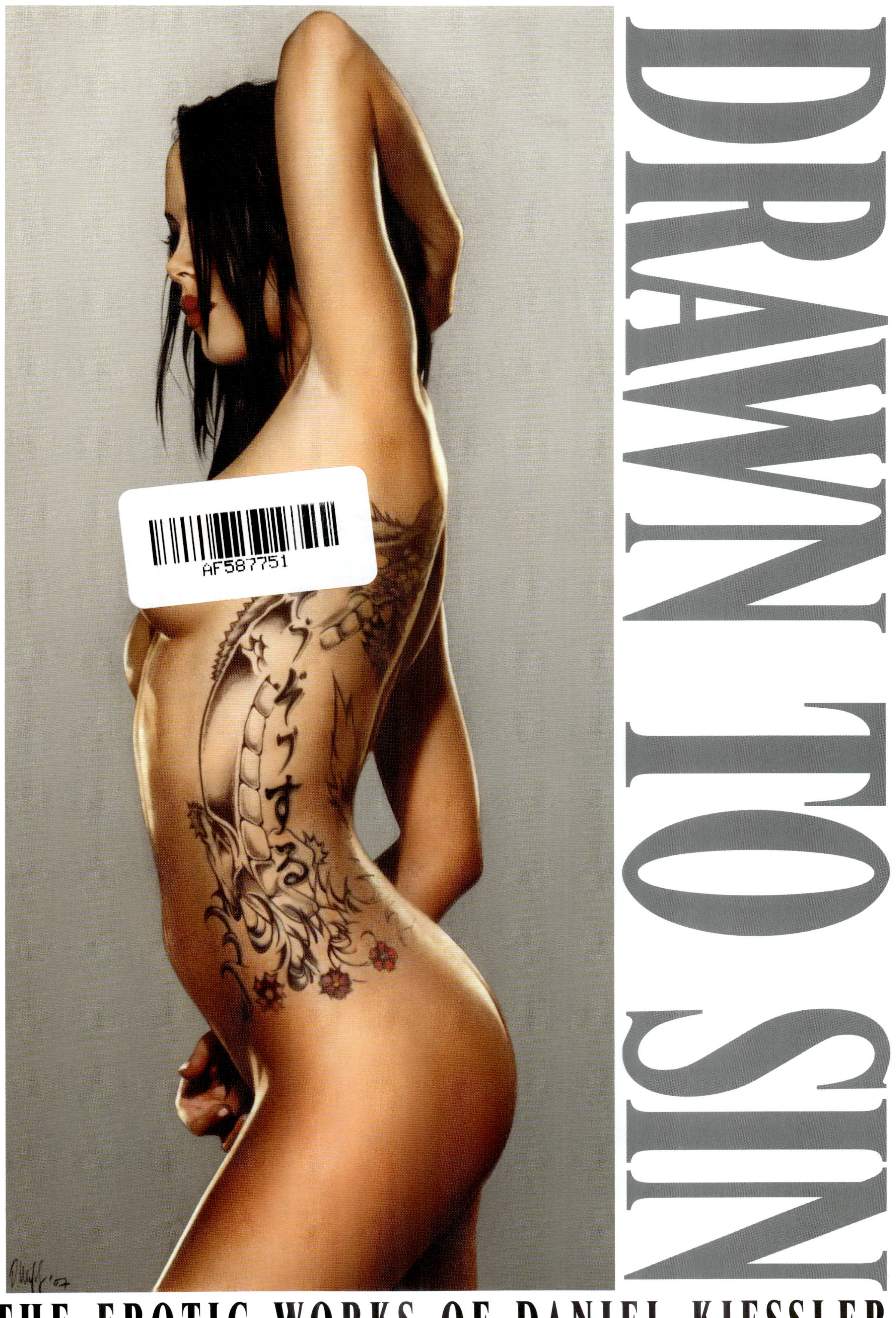

DRAWN TO SIN

THE EROTIC WORKS OF DANIEL KIESSLER

KIESSLER IN KOLOR
NEWER SHADES OF MEANING

This artbook is a collection of images, ideas, sketches and photorealistic works that I've created the past 18 months.

Some images were inspired from photographs that I've collected and archived over the years, but only now have decided to draw them, and most importantly, to see them realized in color.

Color has always been a tool that I avoided for my works with full intention (graphite being my first love). However I *did* have this gallery of images that just cried out to be drawn *and* colored. They would, in fact, *only* work with color.

So, I searched for an artist who could help me create these images and found José August Cano Martinez.

He is one of the most skilled and highly talented colorists I ever had the pleasure to work with. He was the perfect collaborator for this project and transformed my ideas *exactly* the way I wanted to see them for this artistic experiment.

The result is 30 images drawn by me and digitially colored by José and some selected solo graphite works of mine.

I hope you enjoy the book. Color me pleased!

Daniel Kiessler

Düsseldorf, August 2010

Drawn to Sin
The Erotic Art Works of Daniel Kiessler

Printed in Hong Kong.
Book design by Grassy Knoll Studios.

Published by
SQP Inc.
PO Box 248 - Columbus, NJ 08022

Sal Quartuccio & Bob Keenan - Publishers

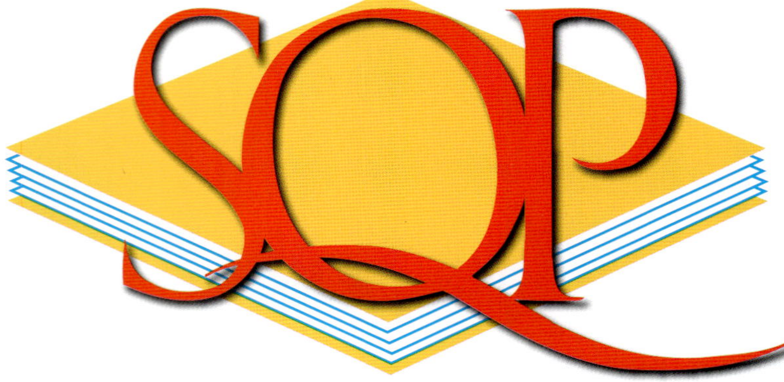

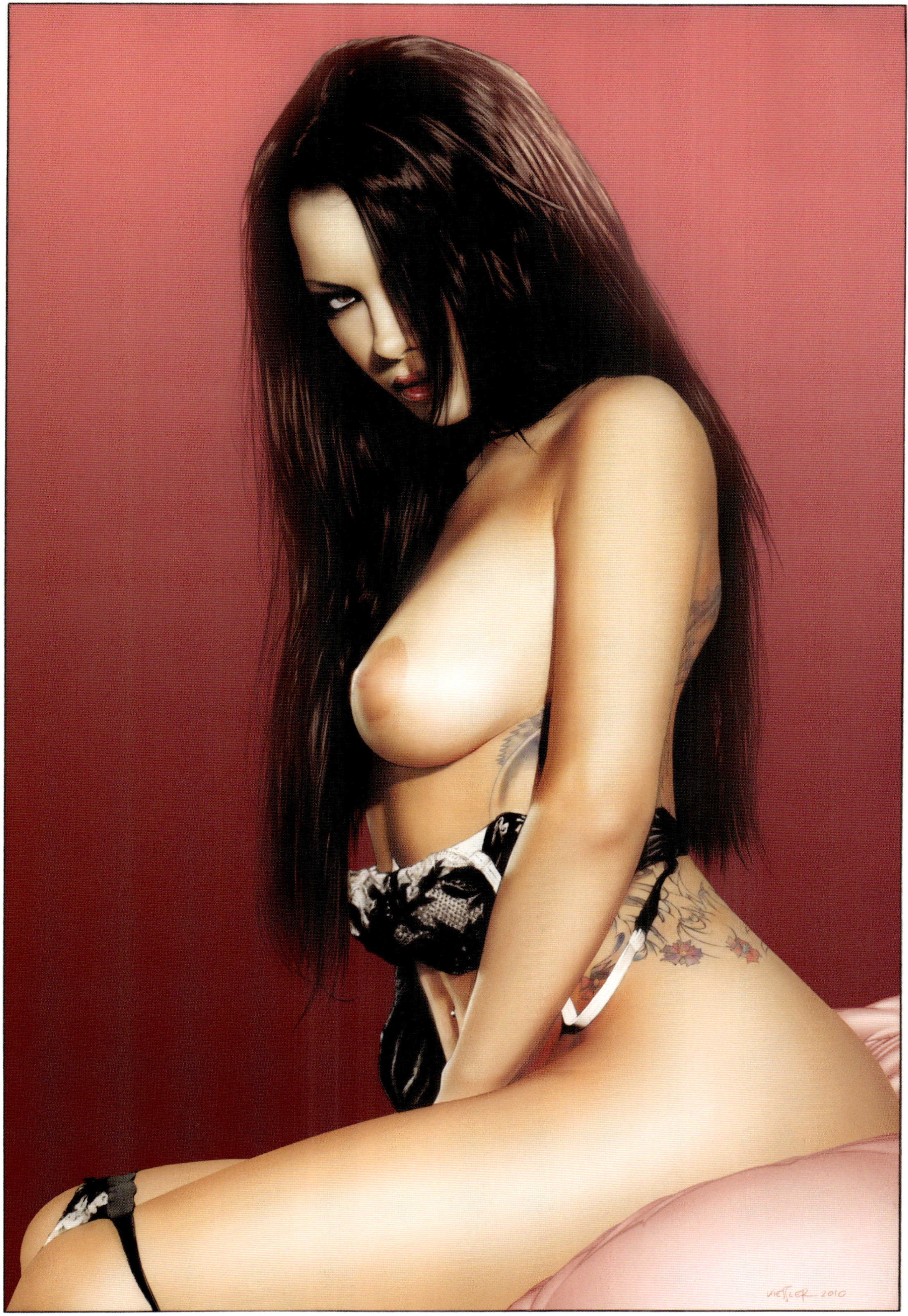

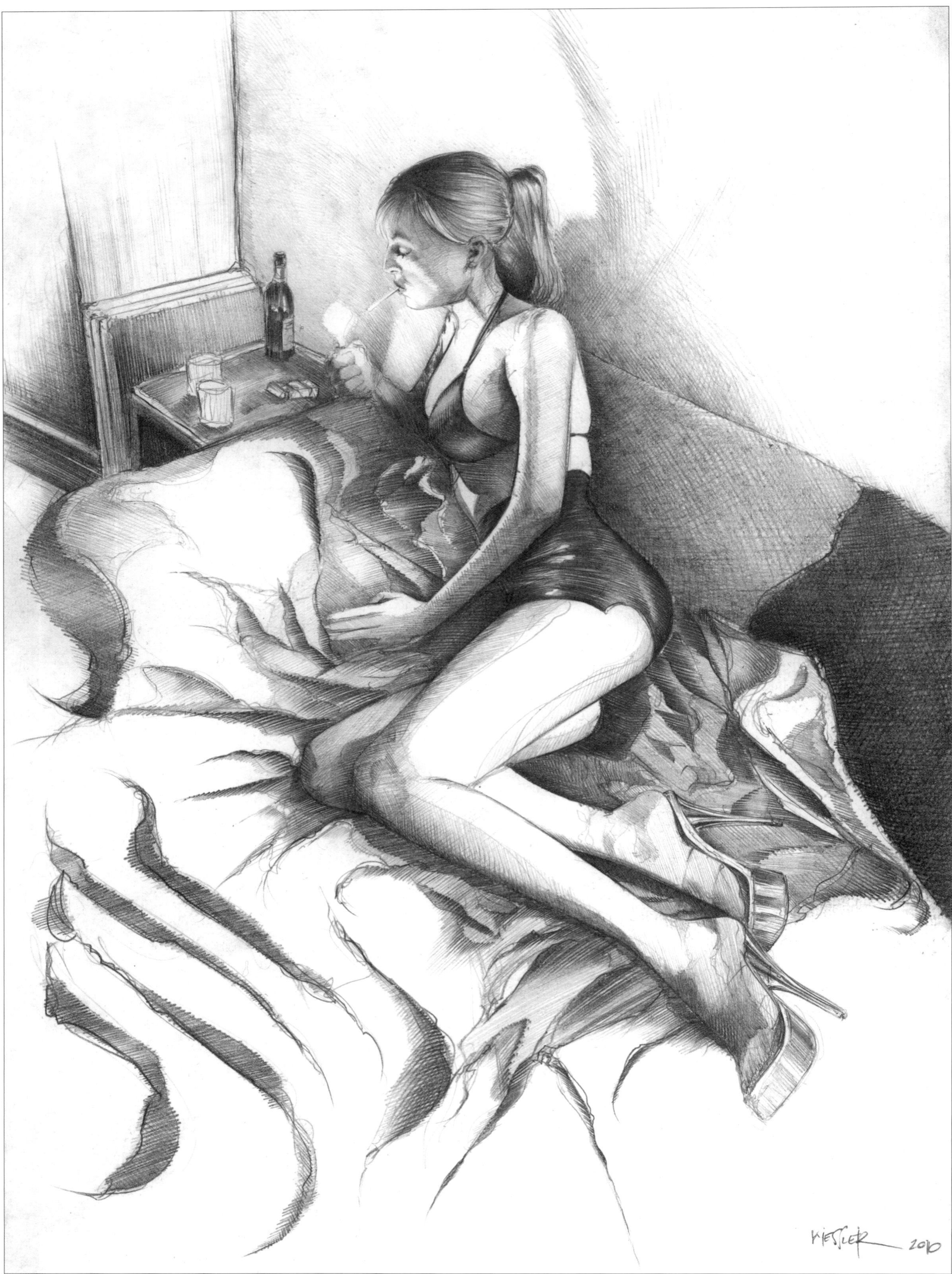

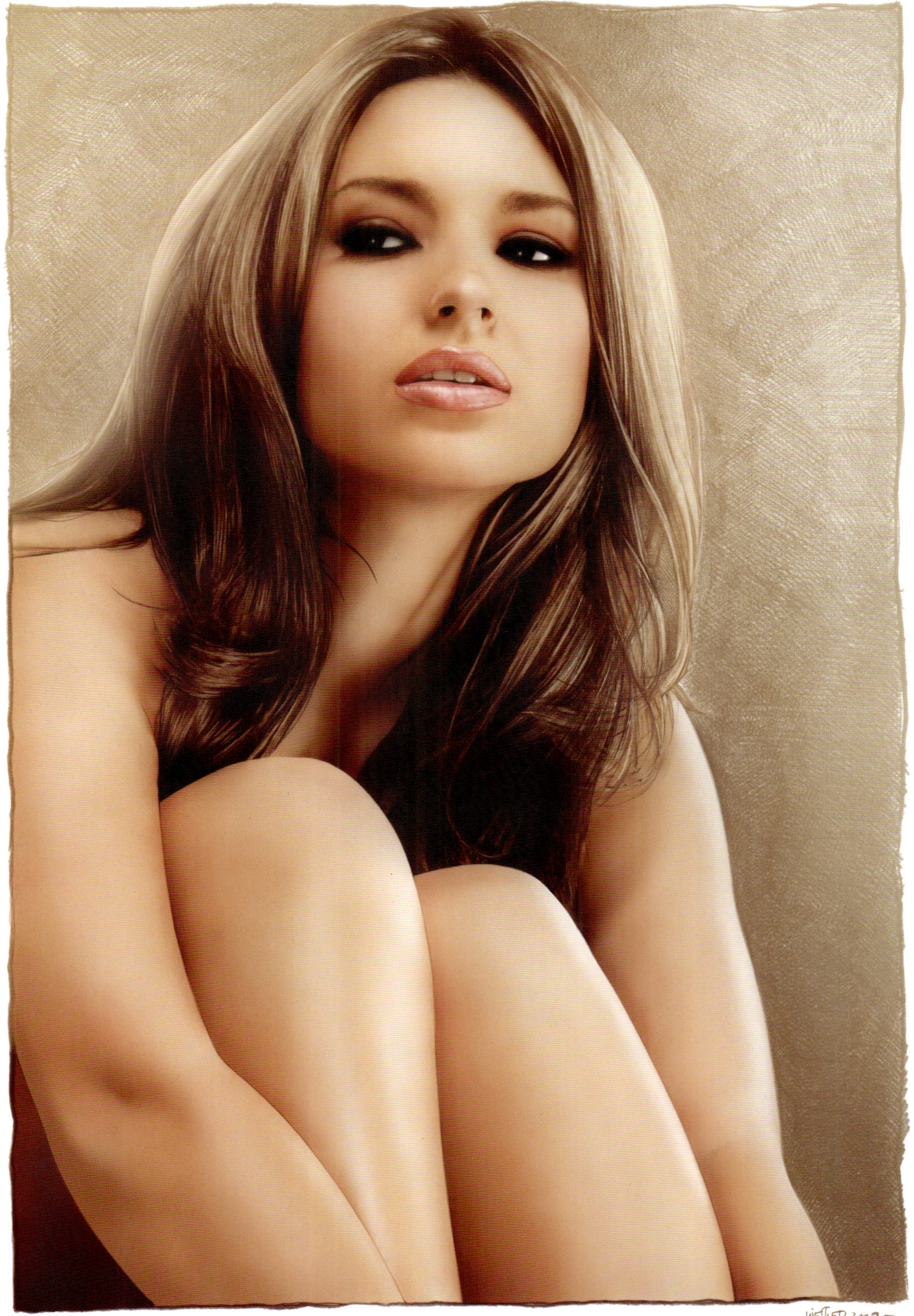

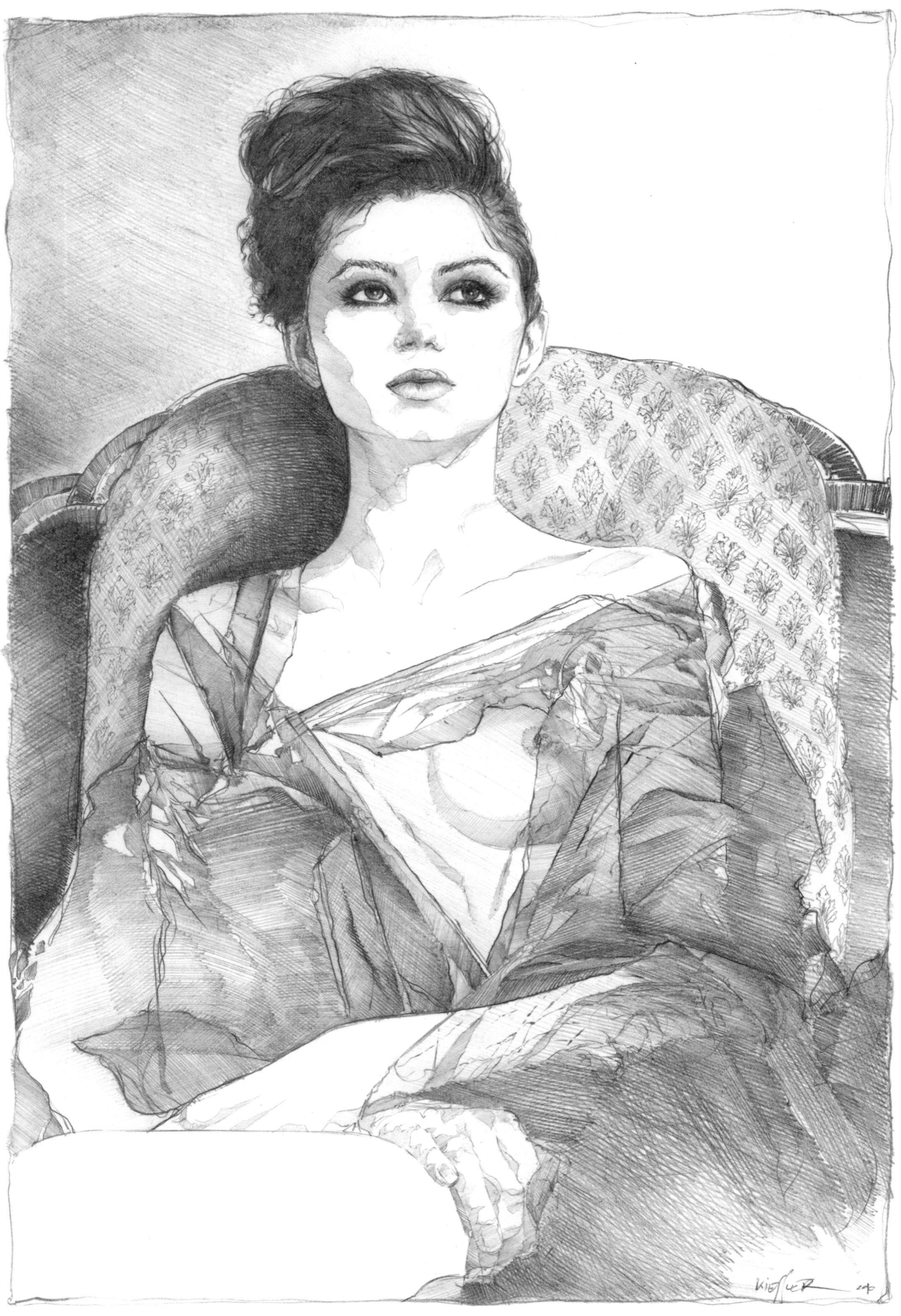

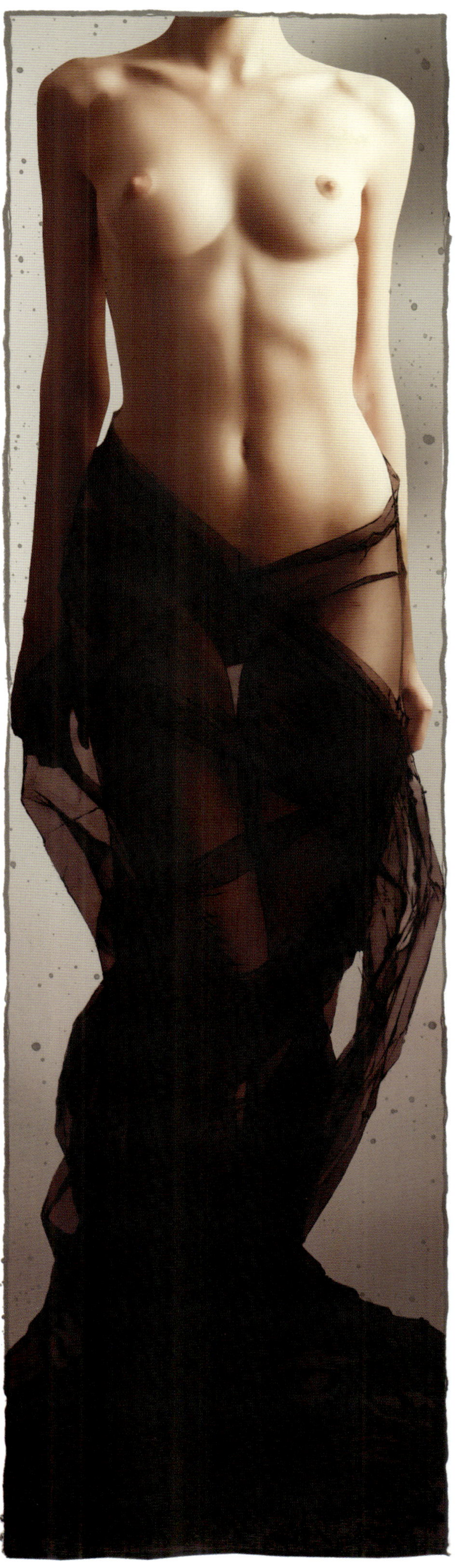

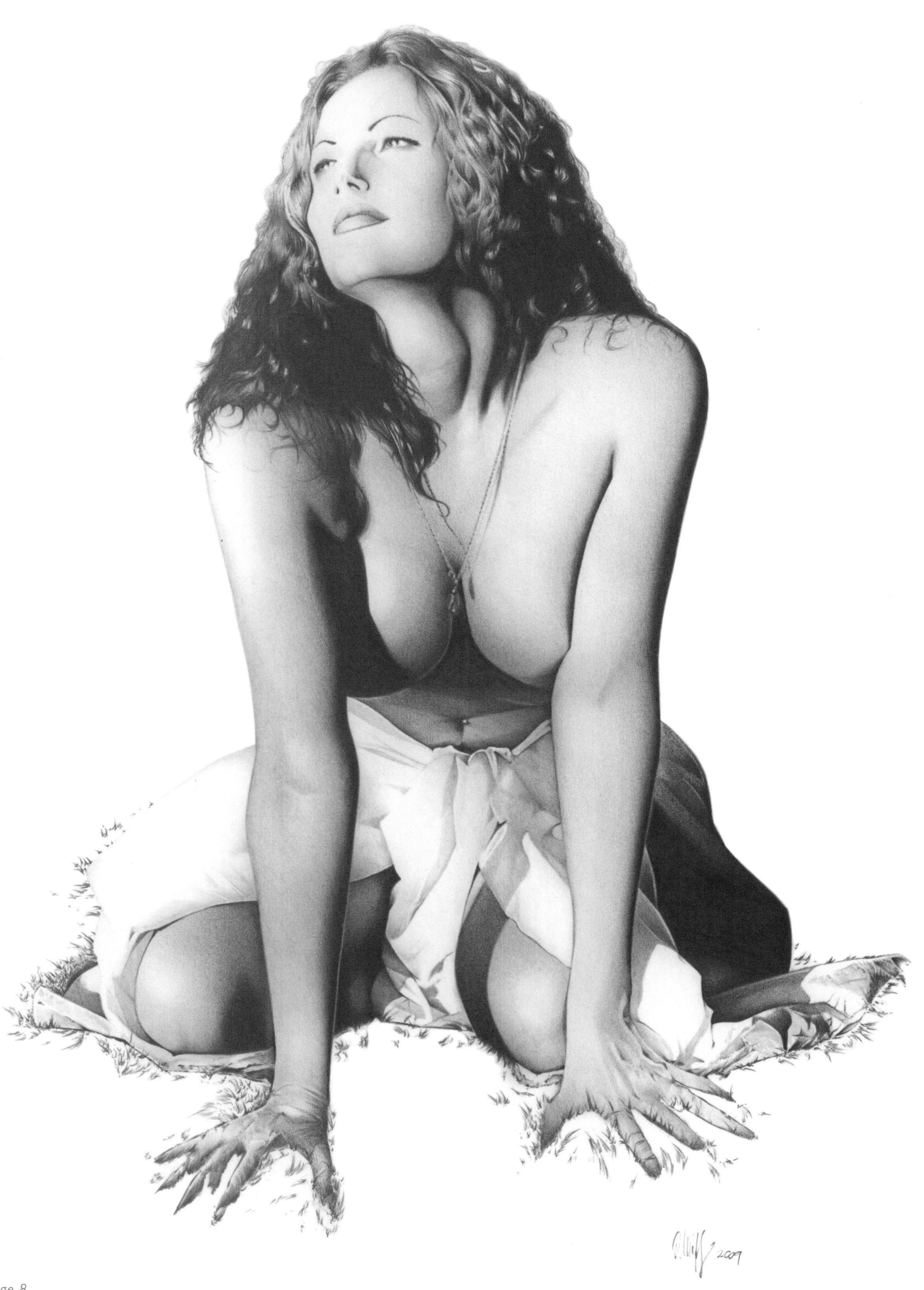

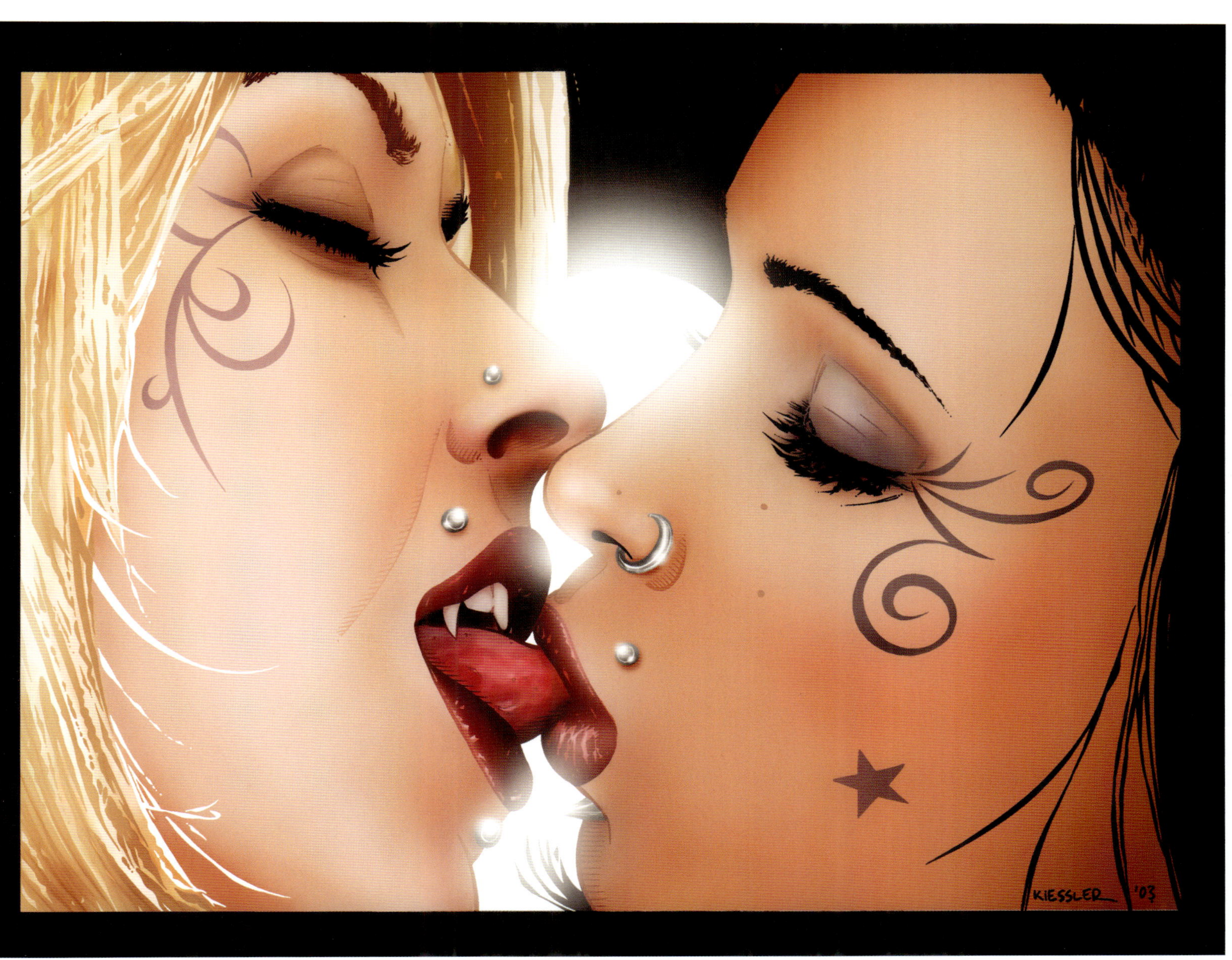
KIESSLER '03

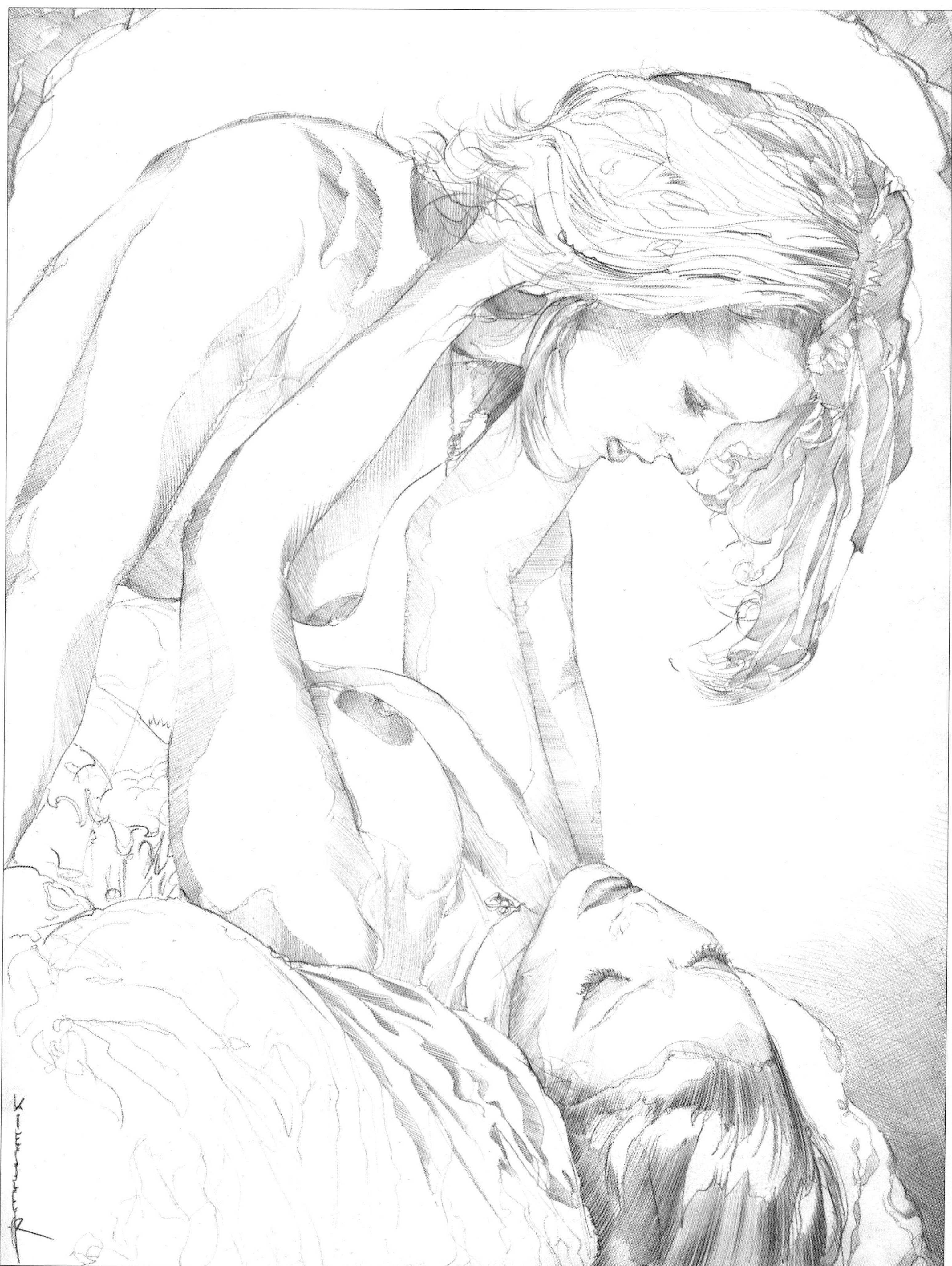

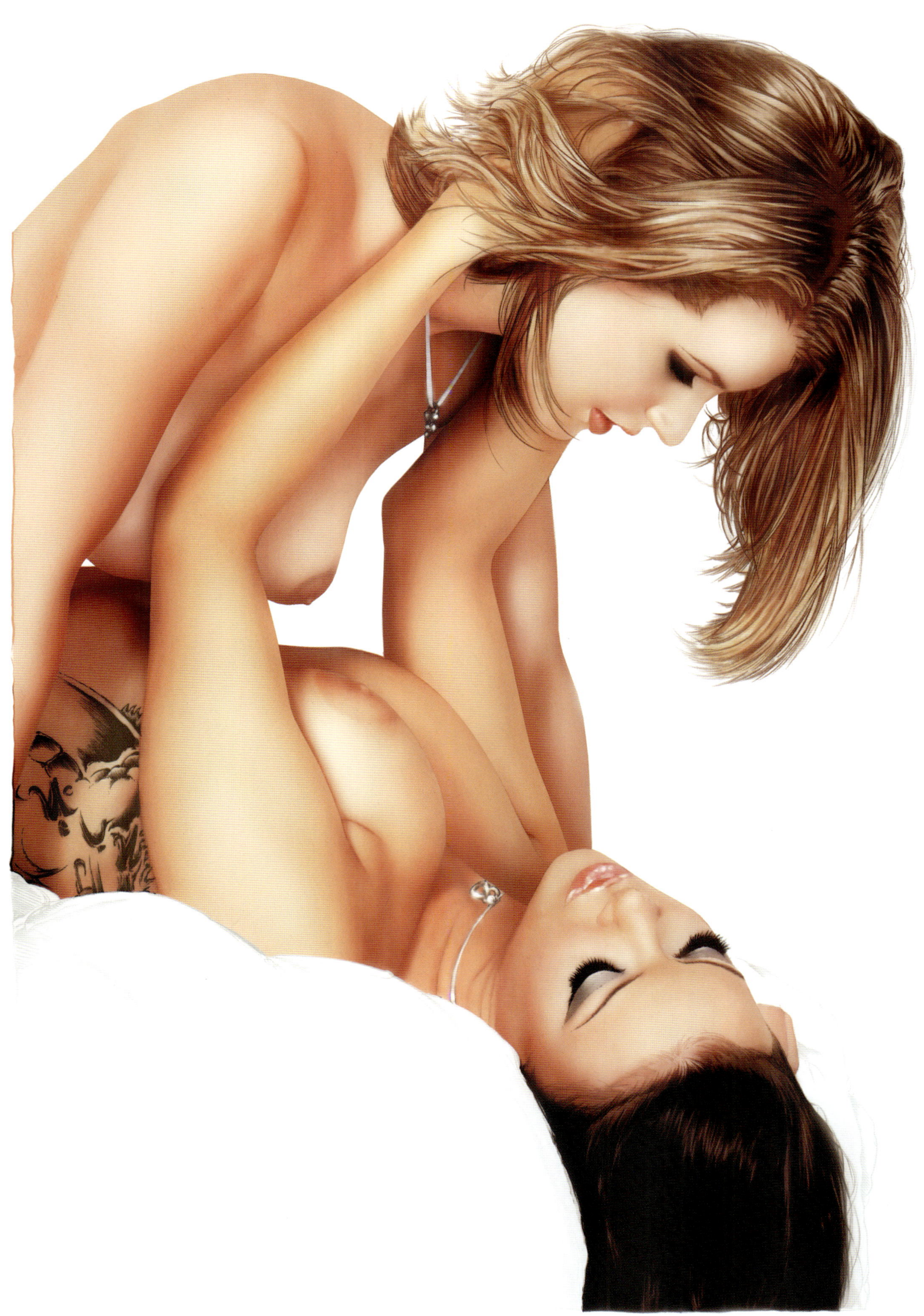

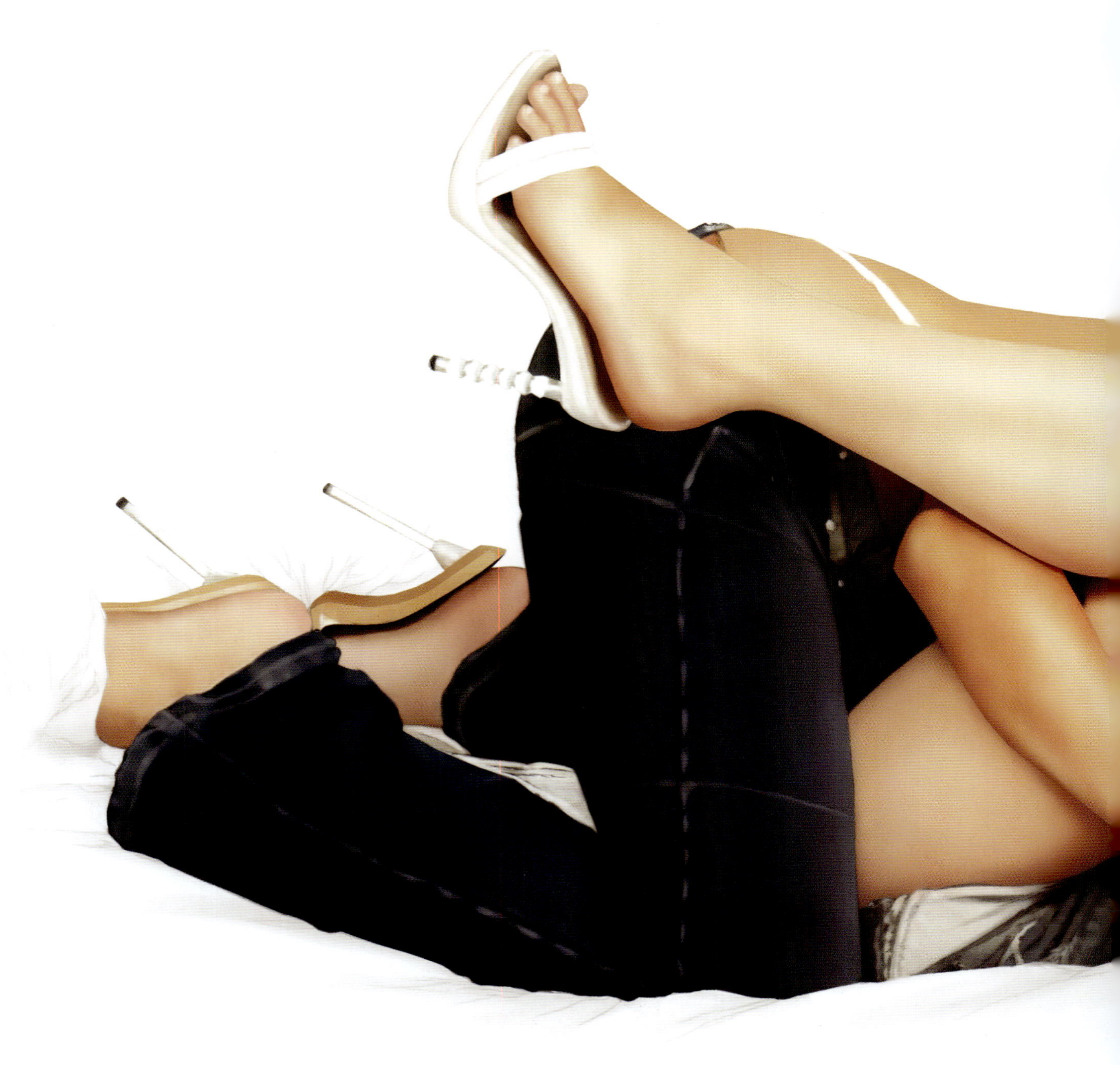

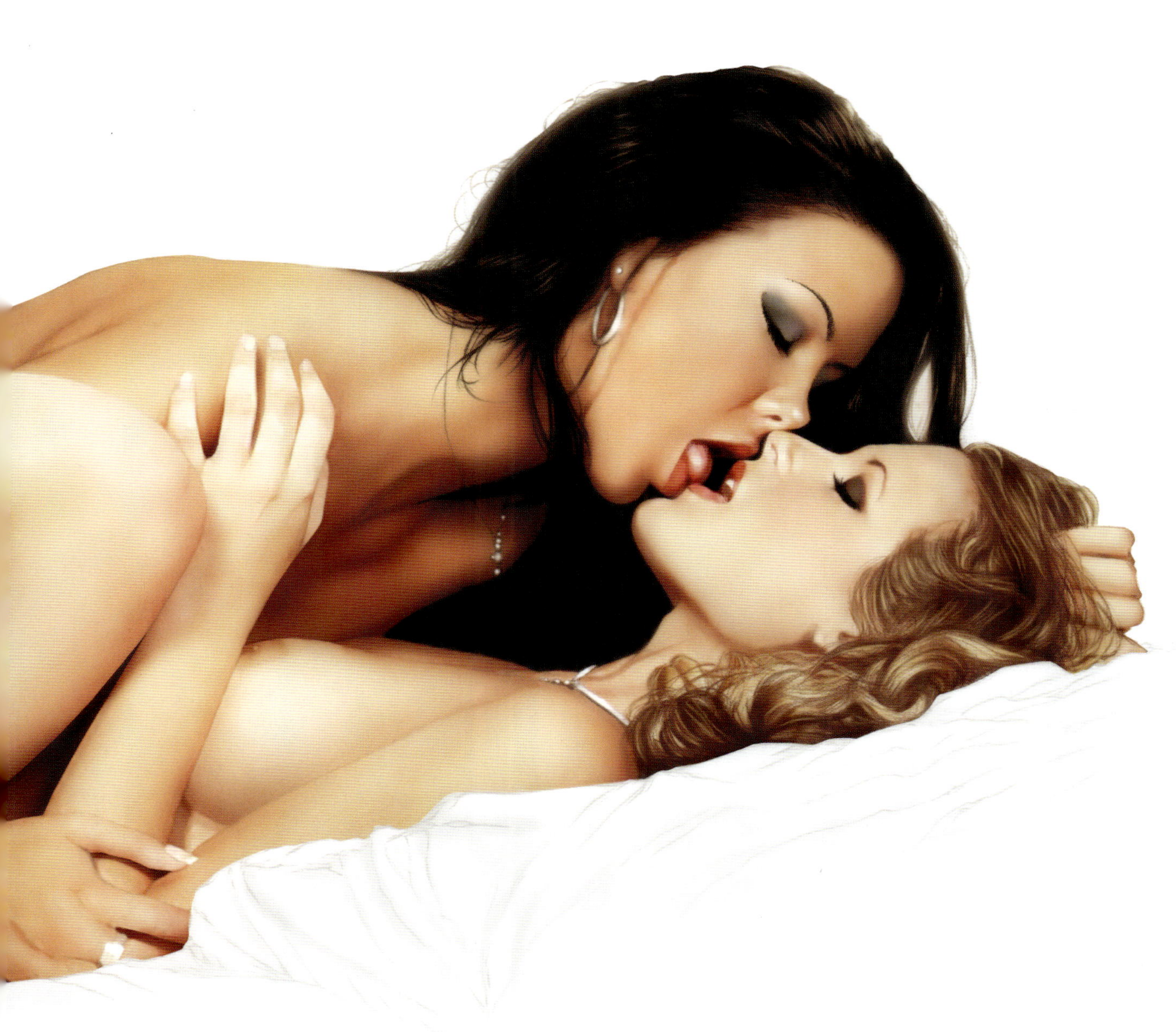

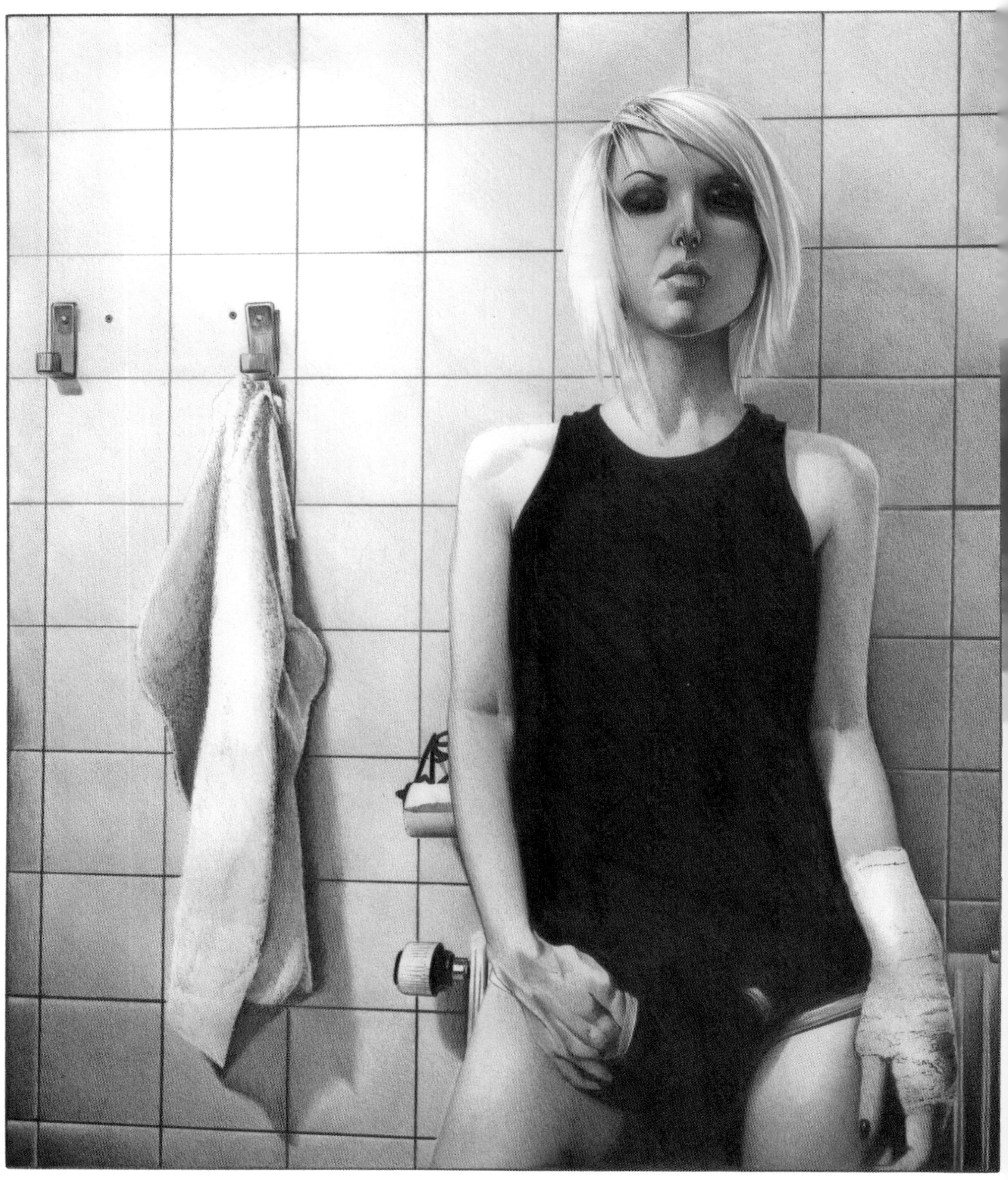

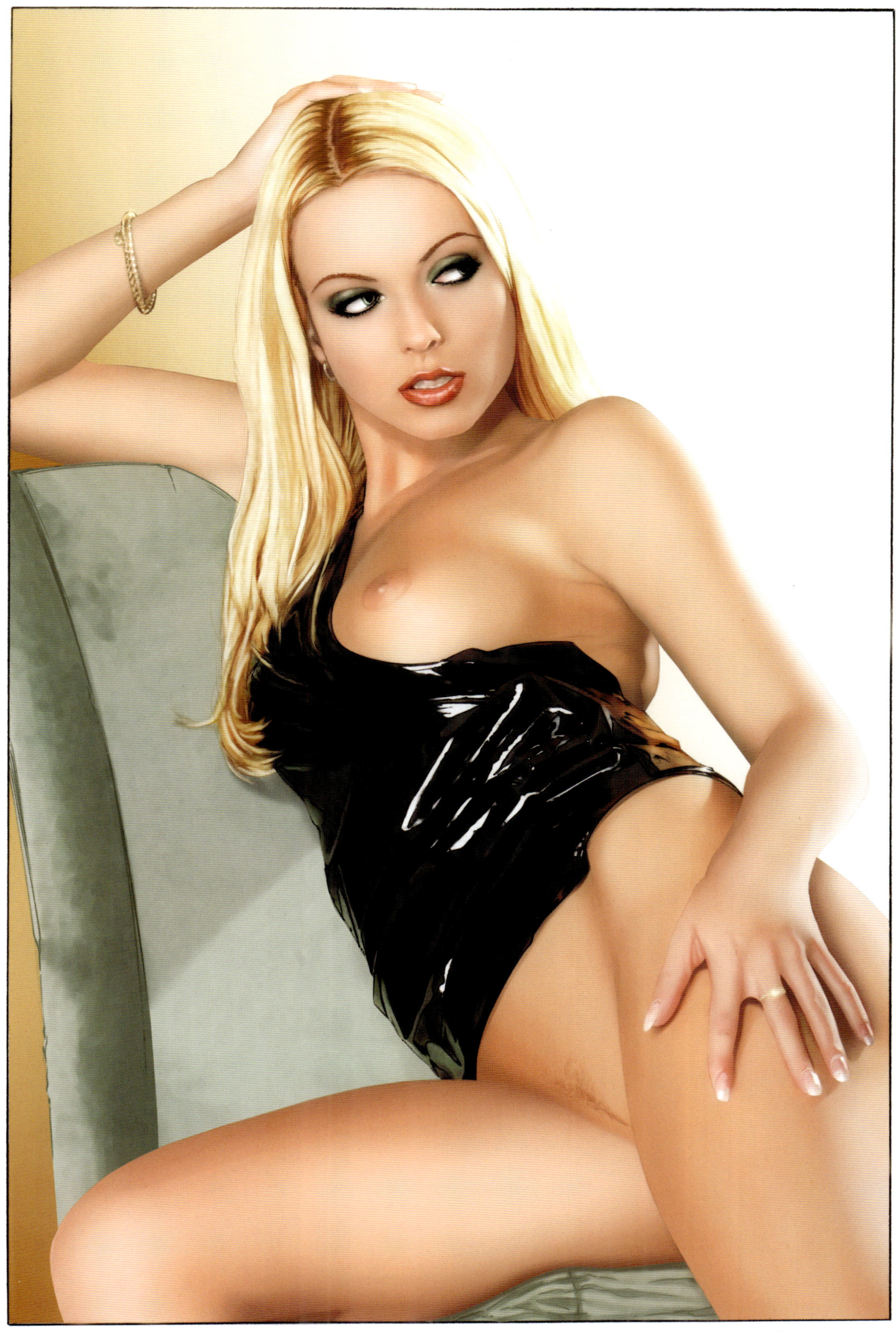
KIESSLER 2010

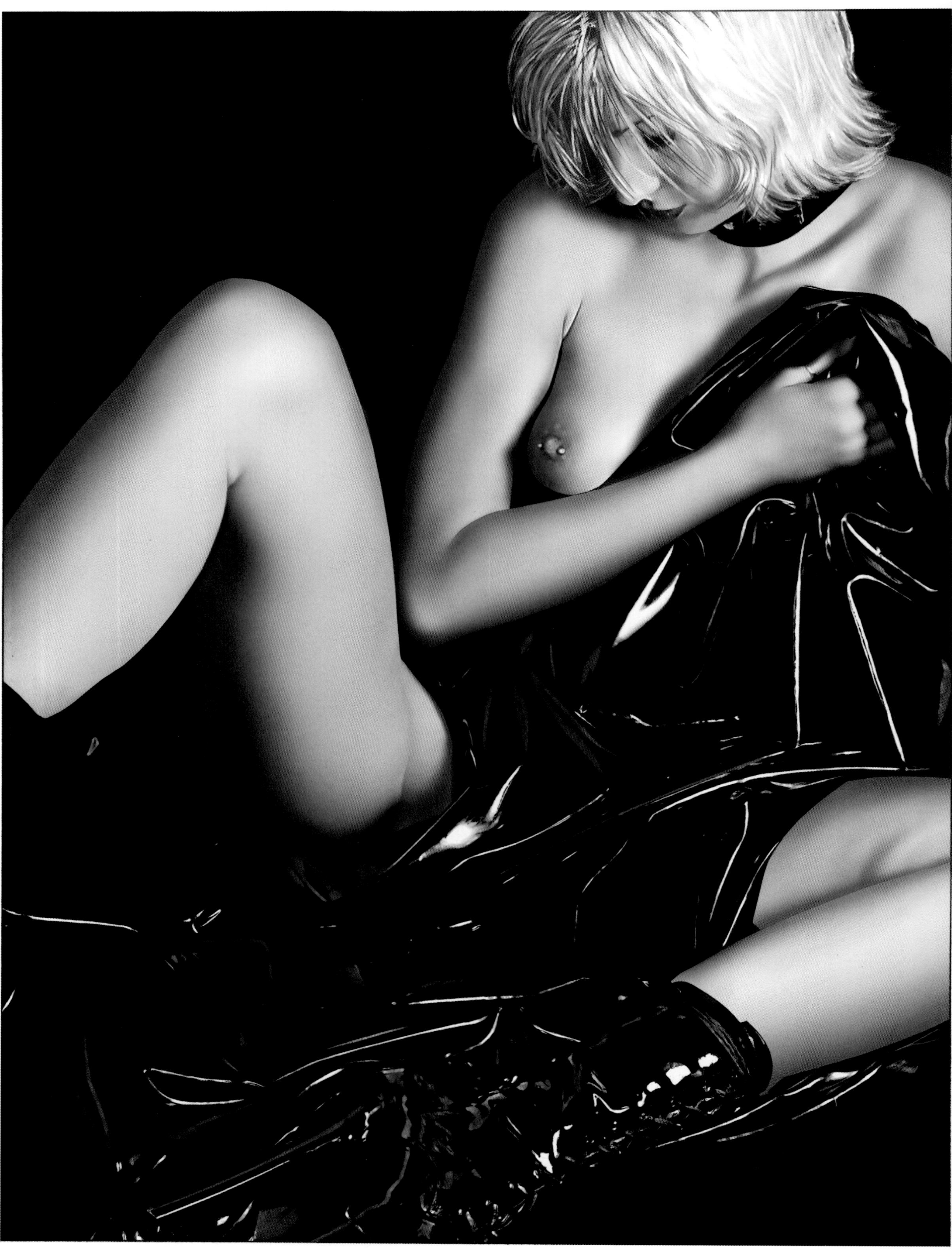

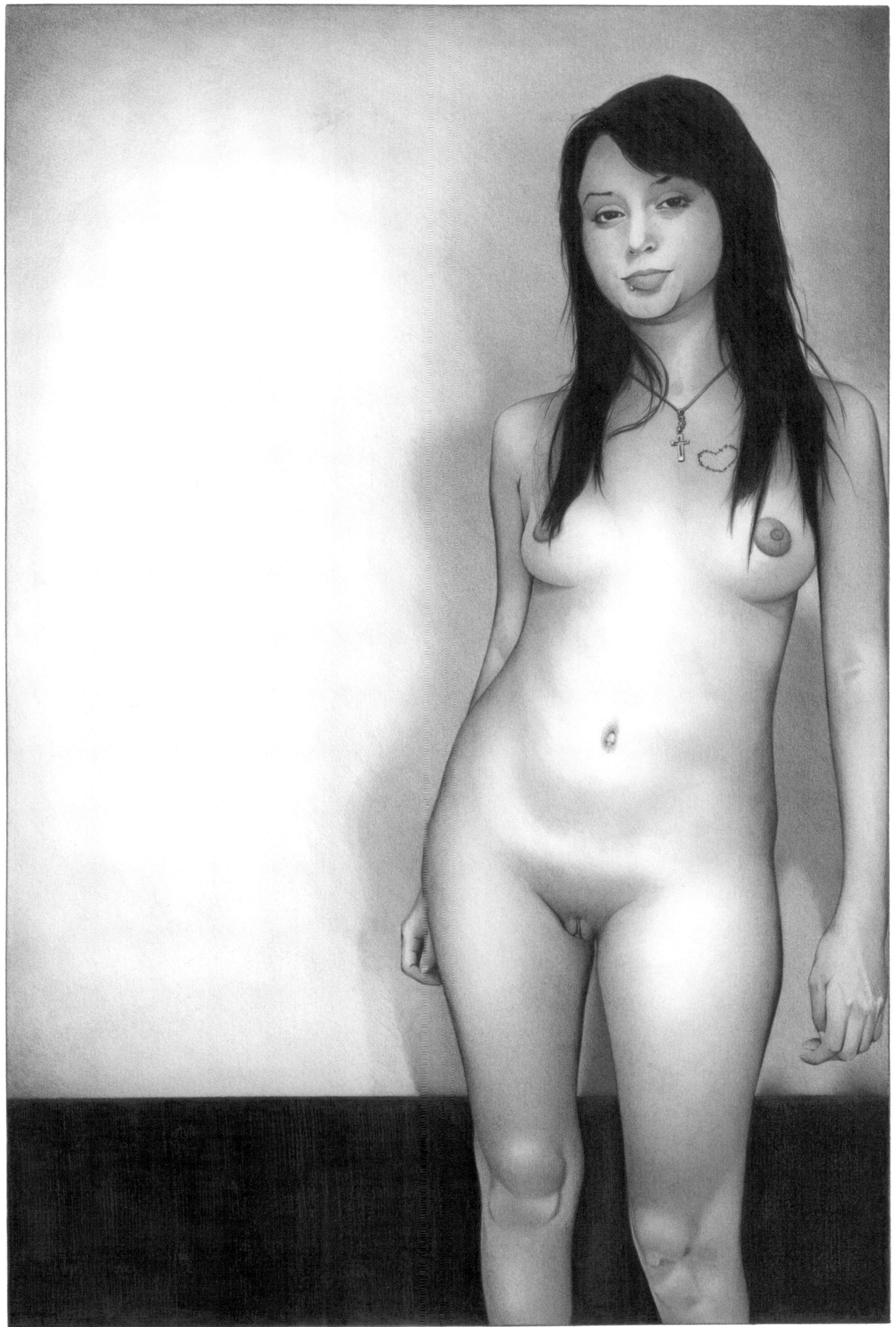

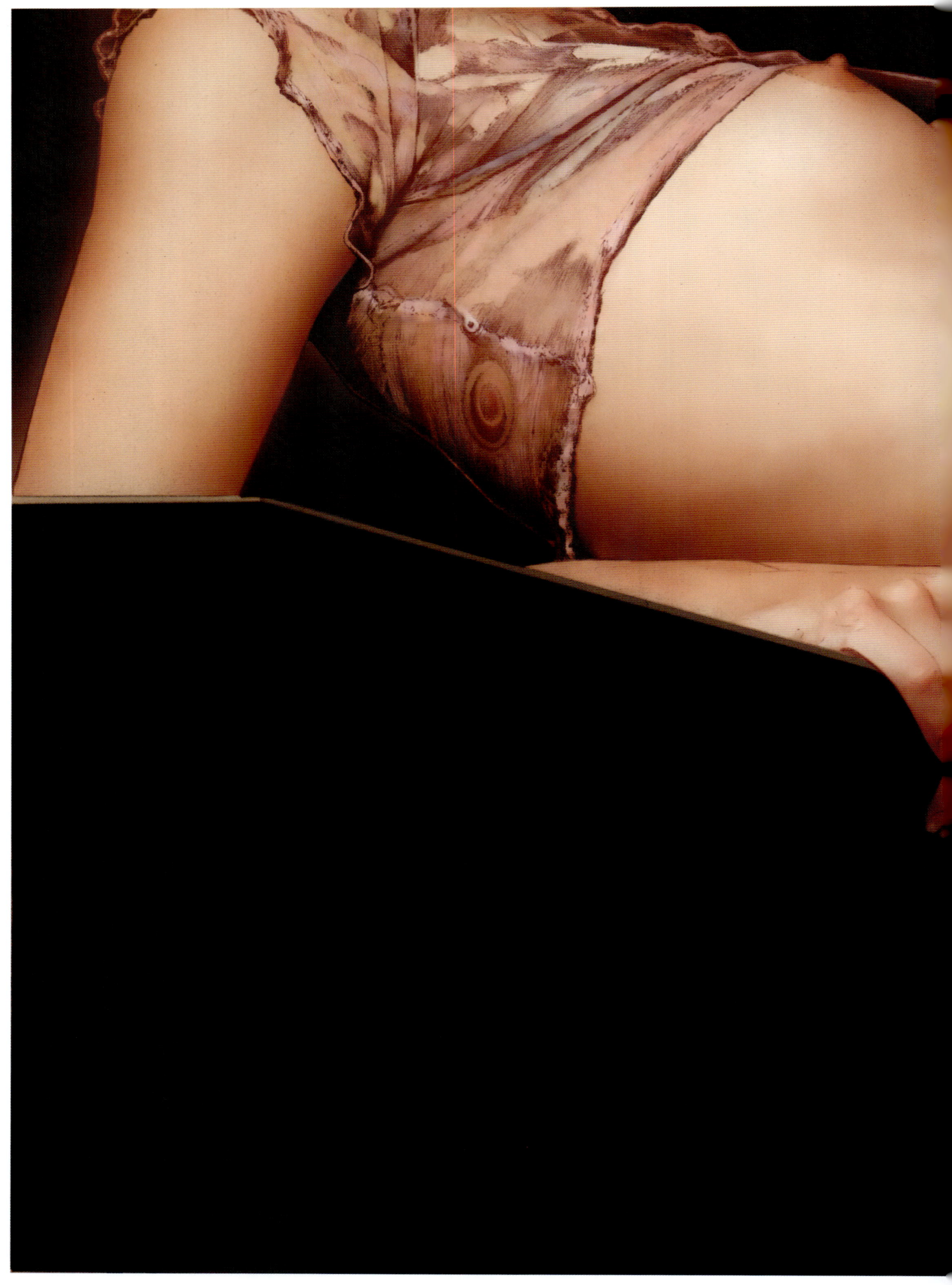

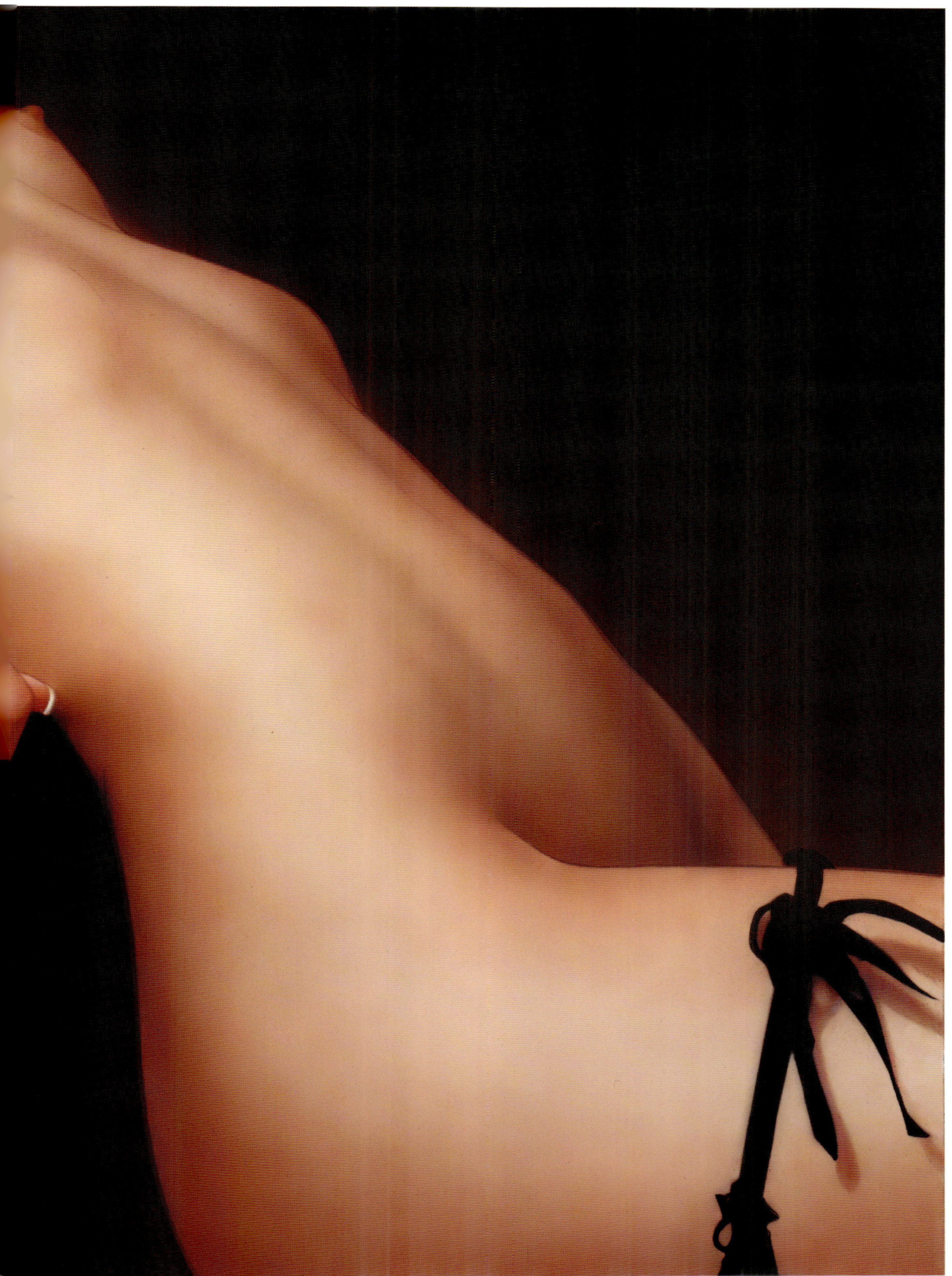

WESSLER 2007

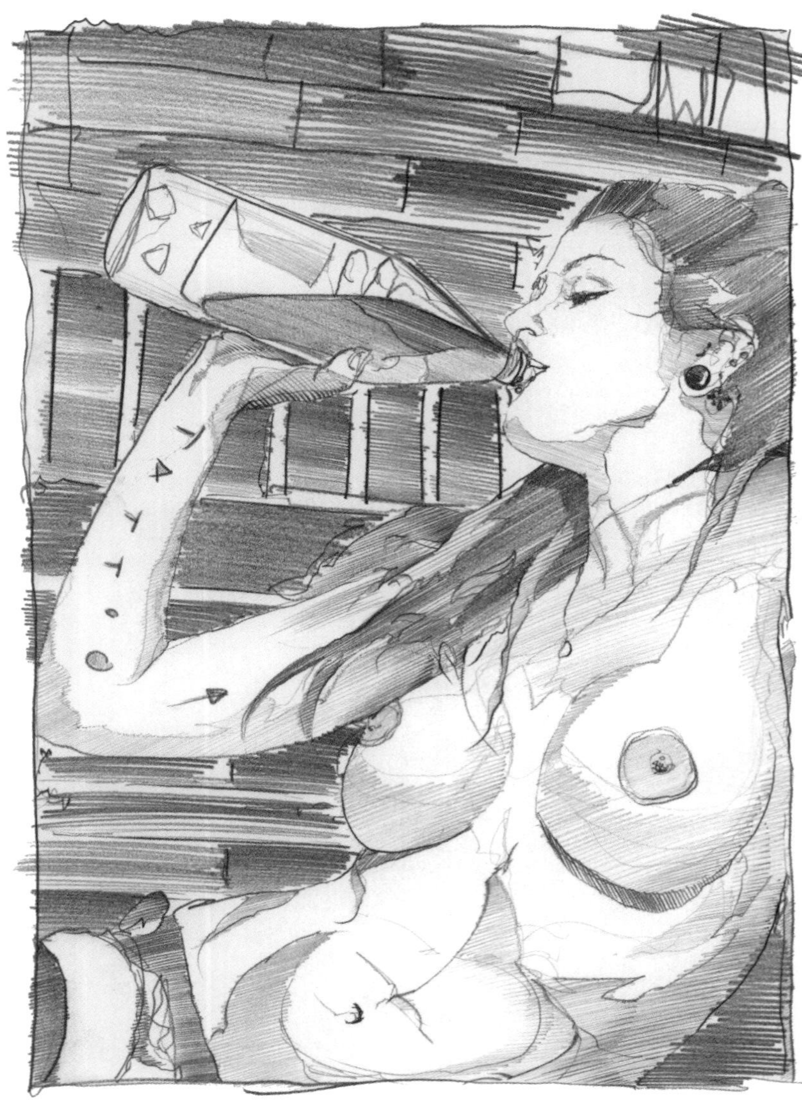

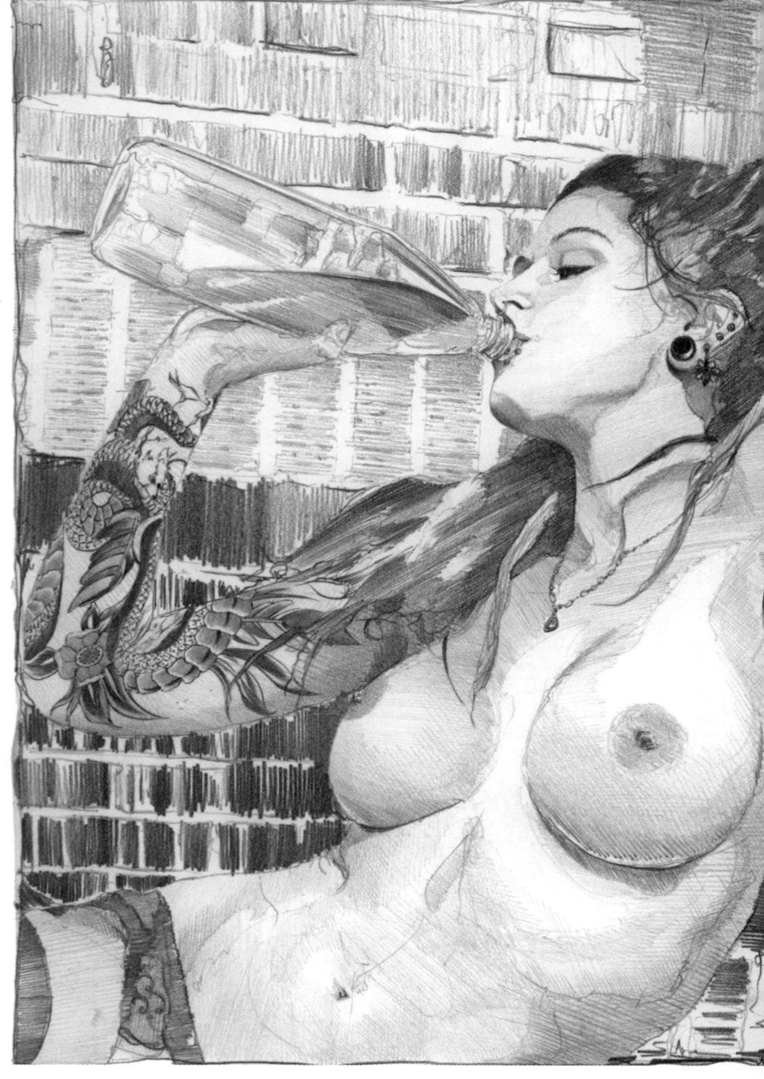

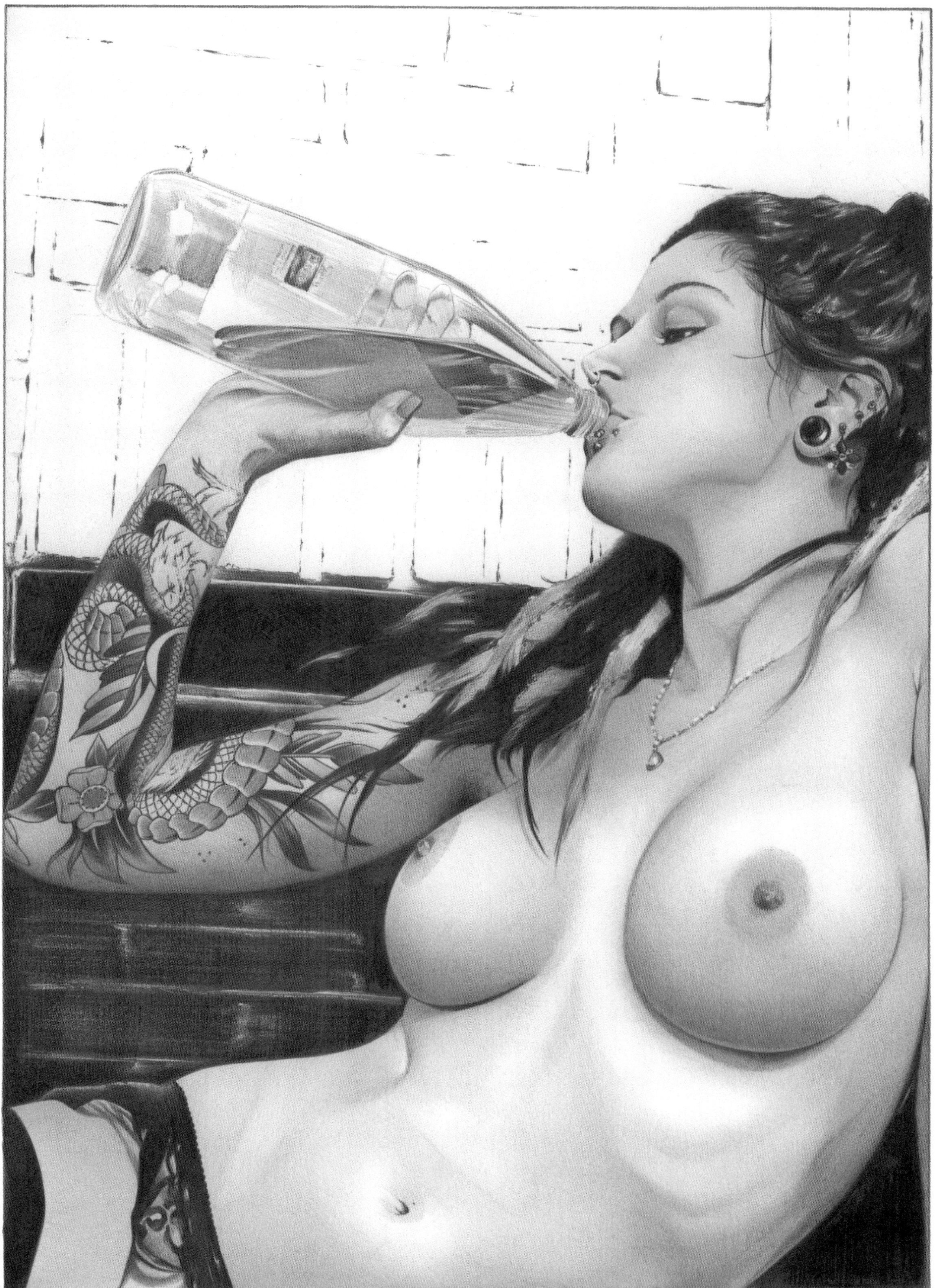

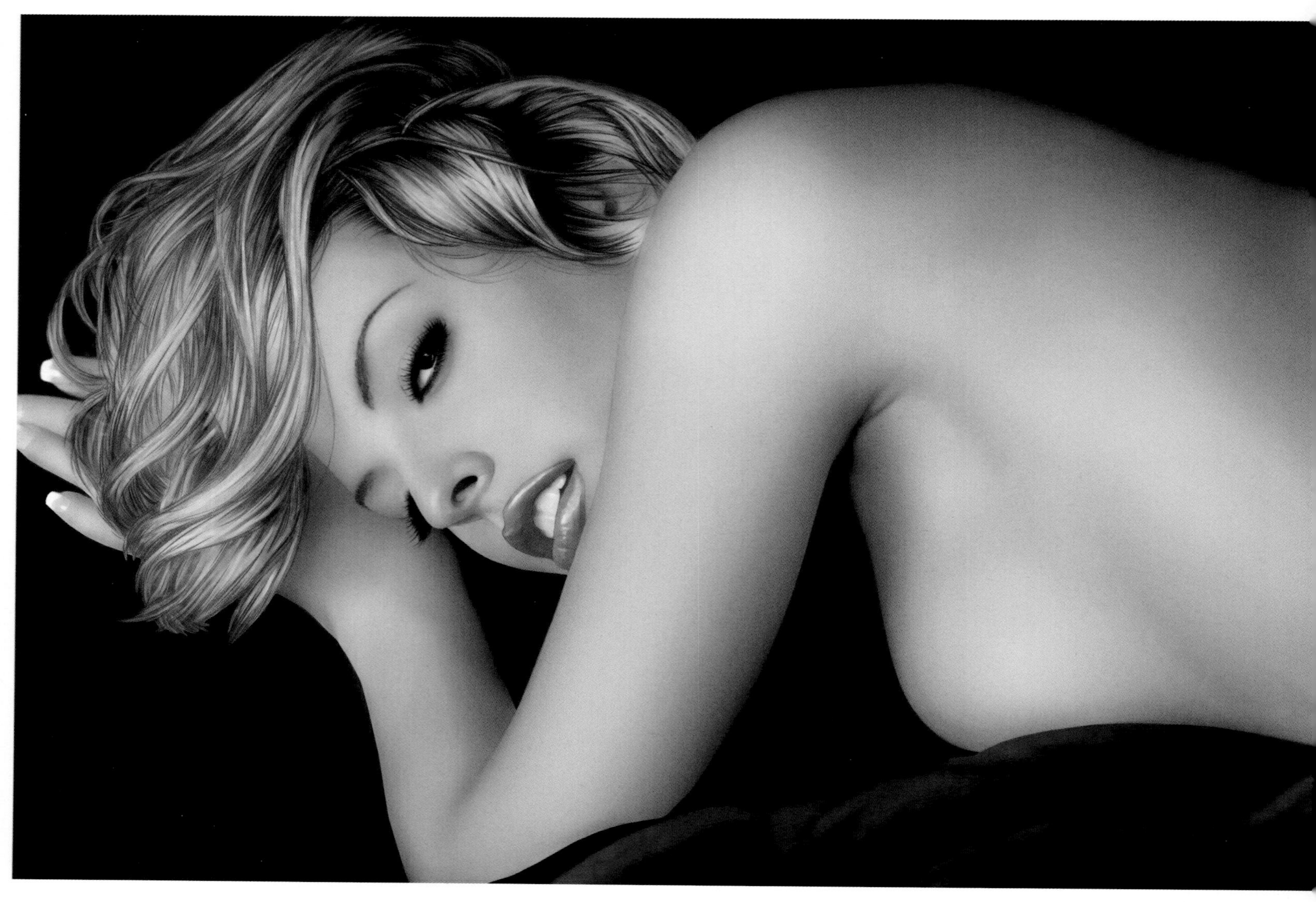

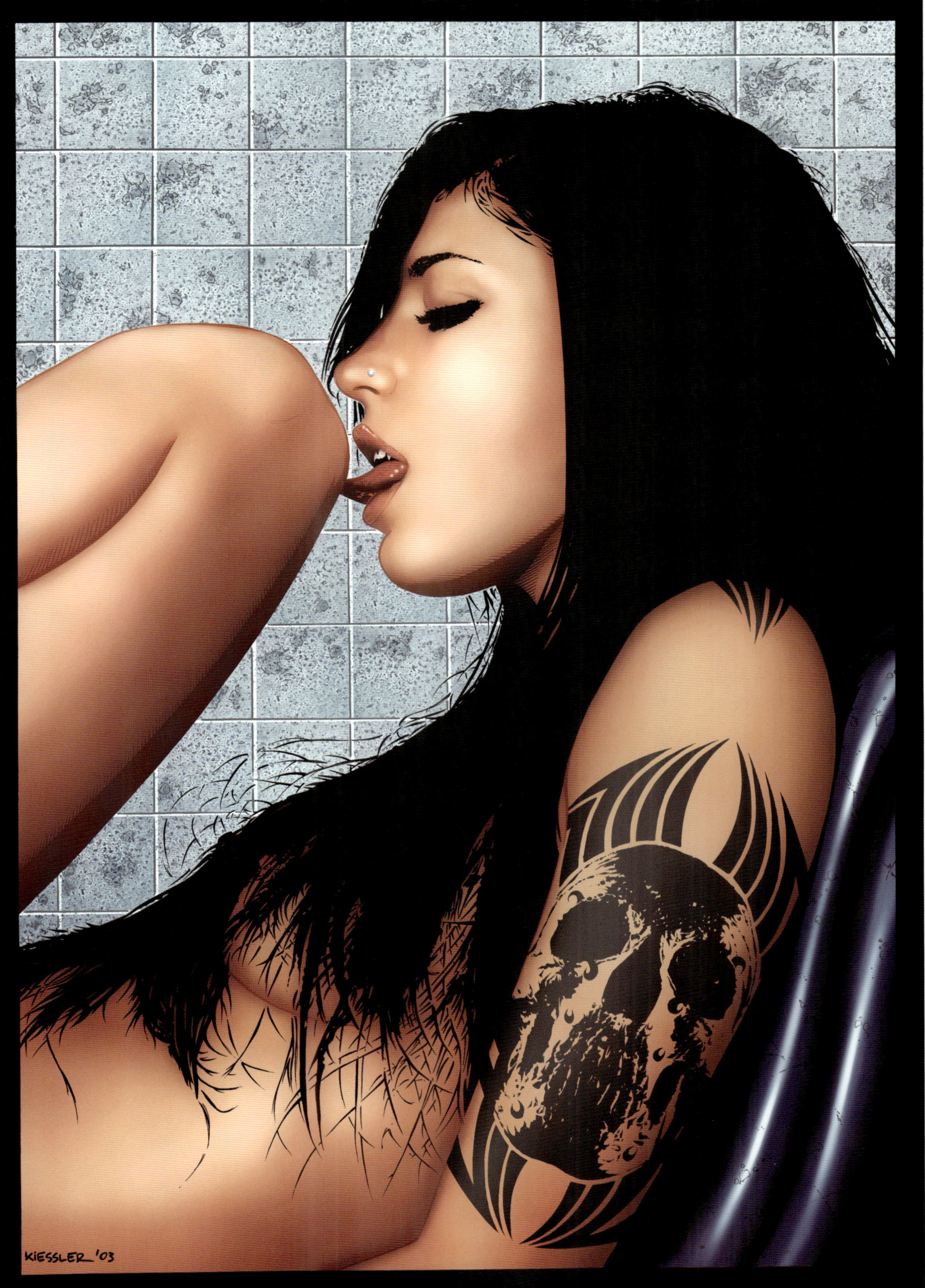
KIESSLER '03

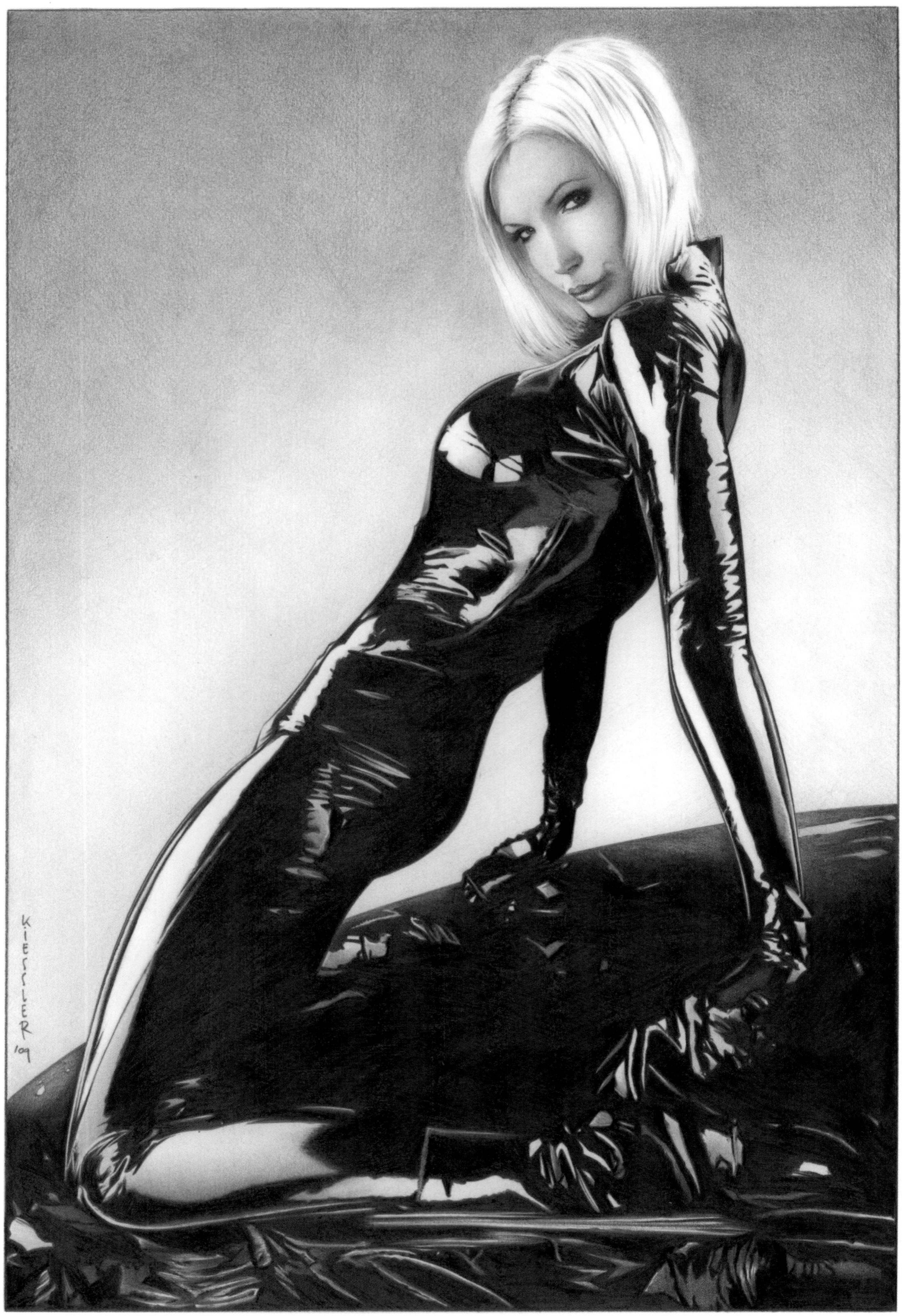
KIESSLER
'09

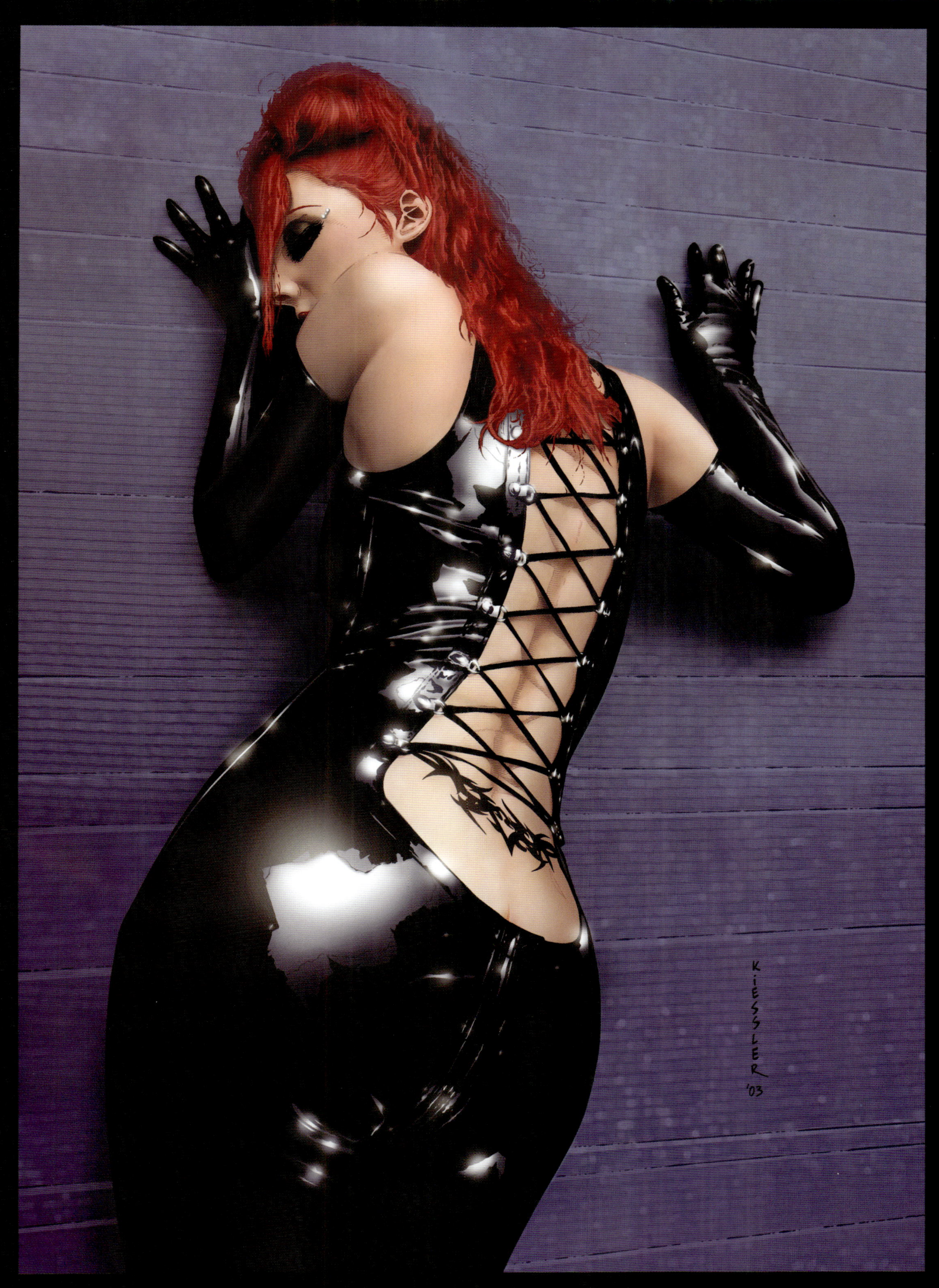
KIESSLER
'03

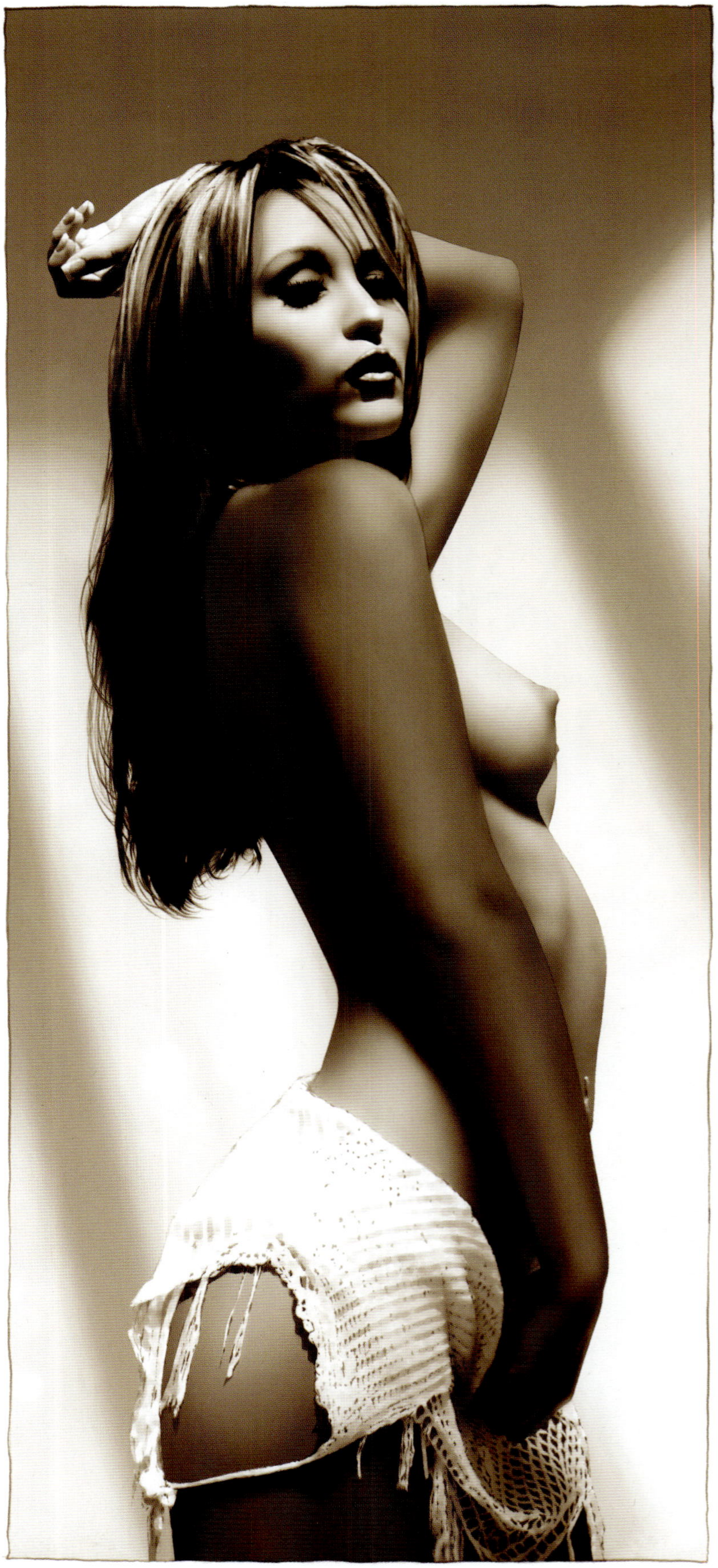

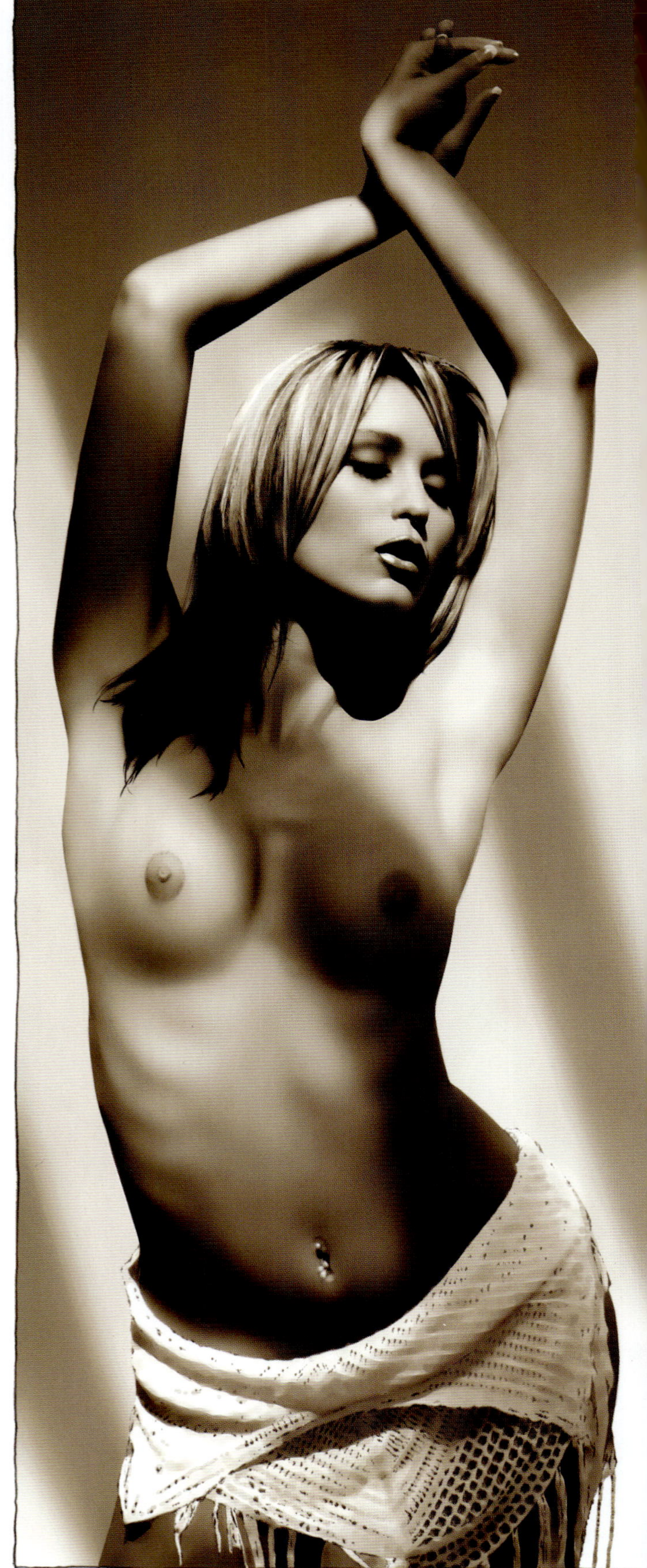

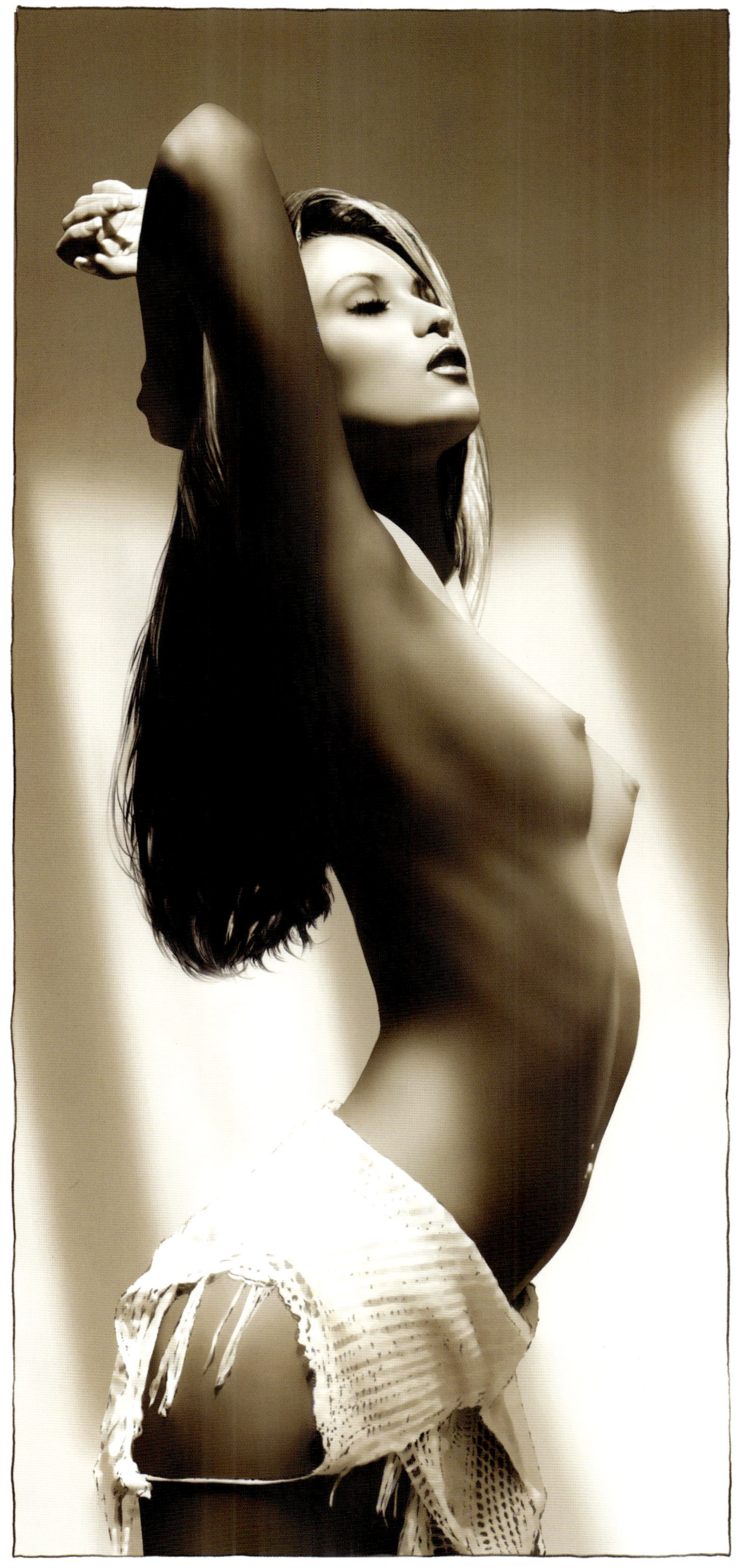

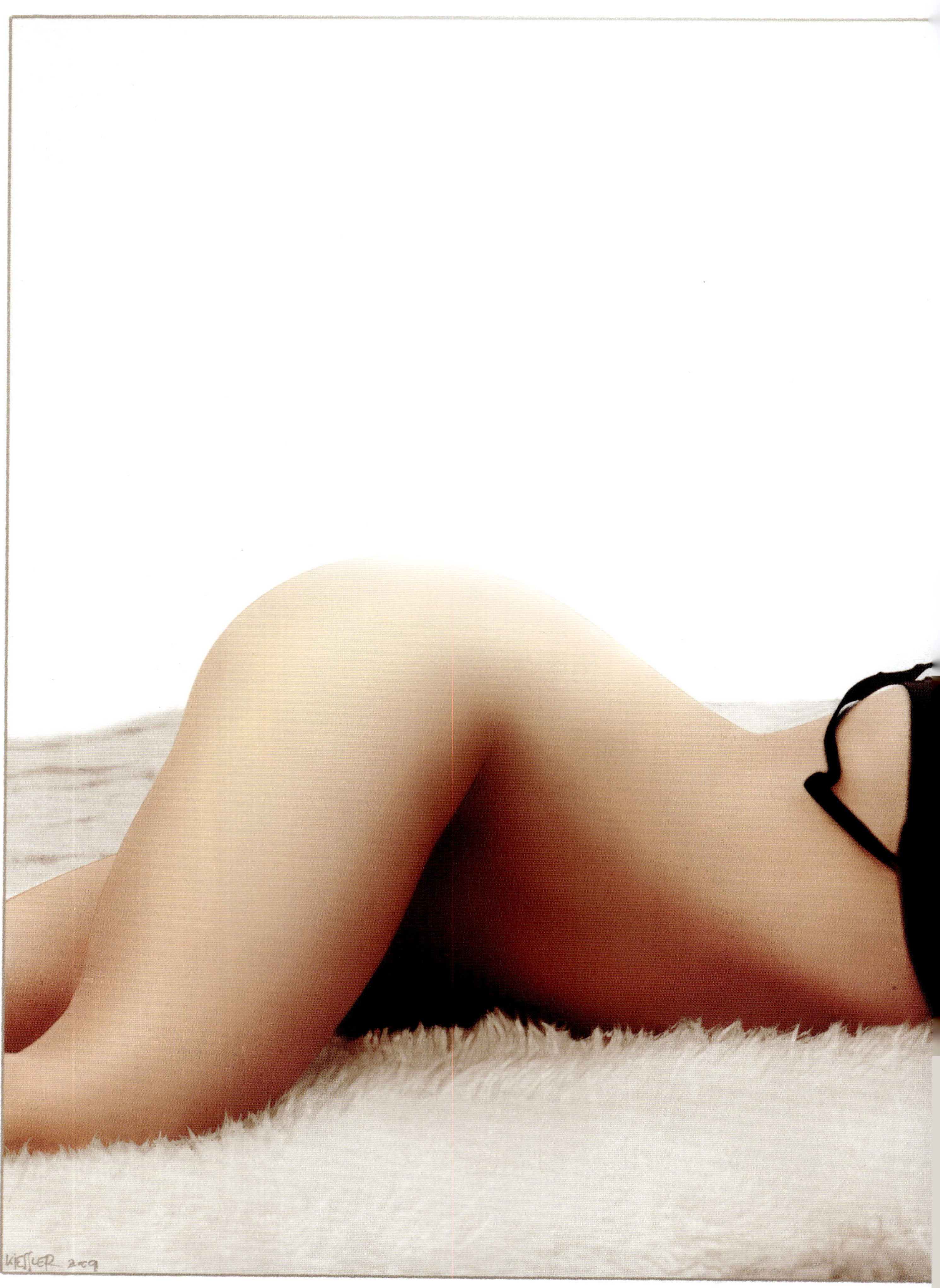

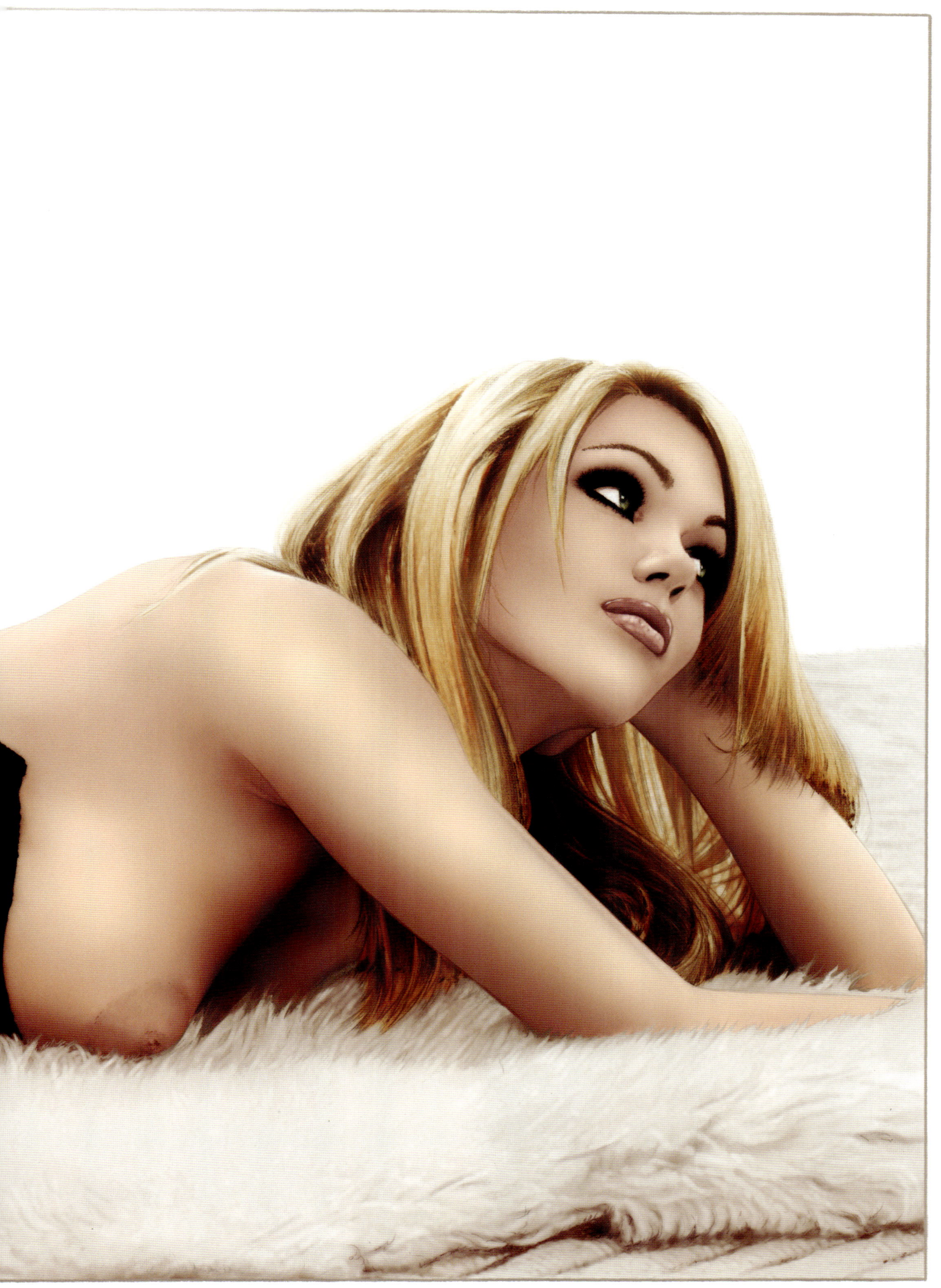

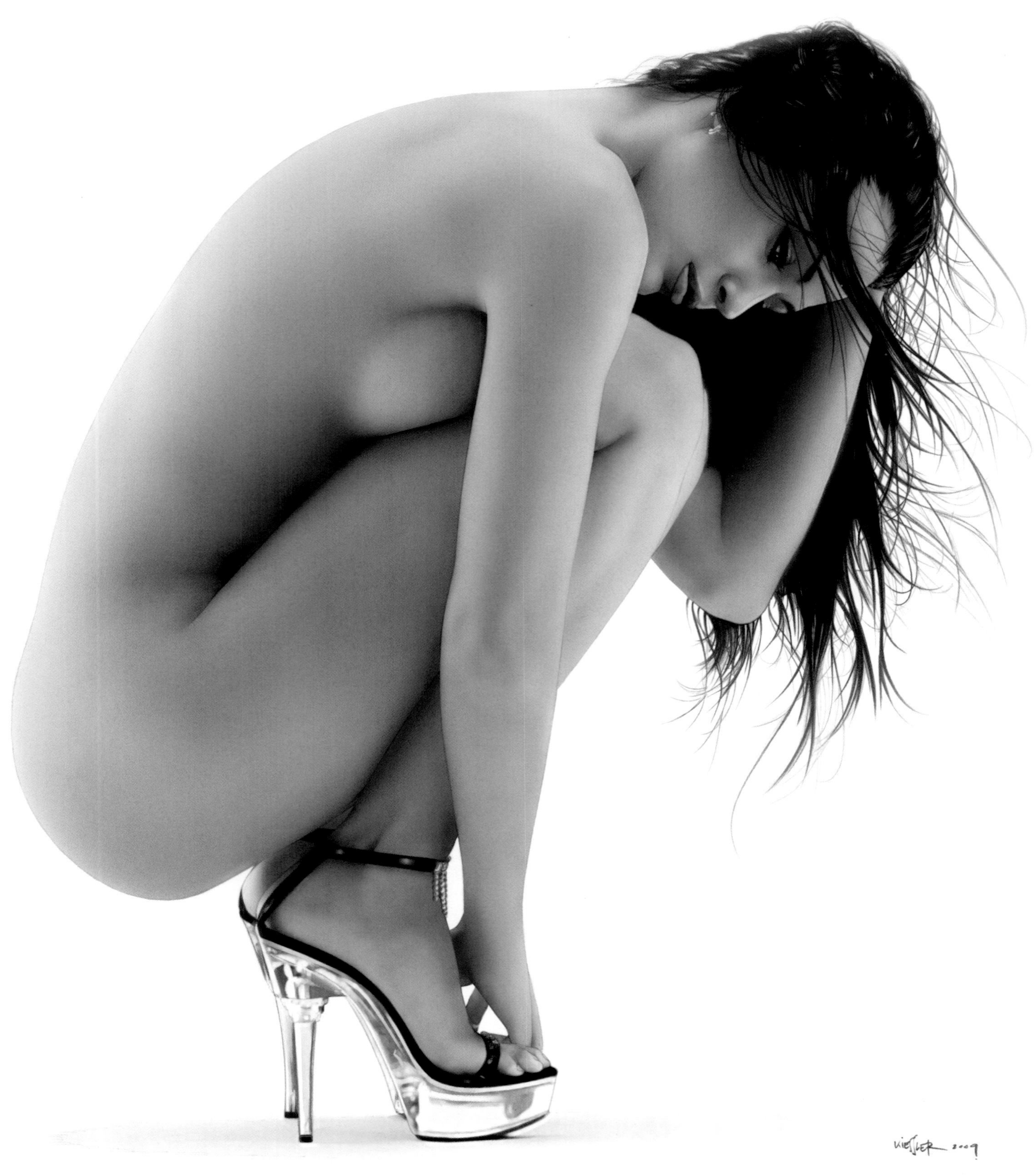

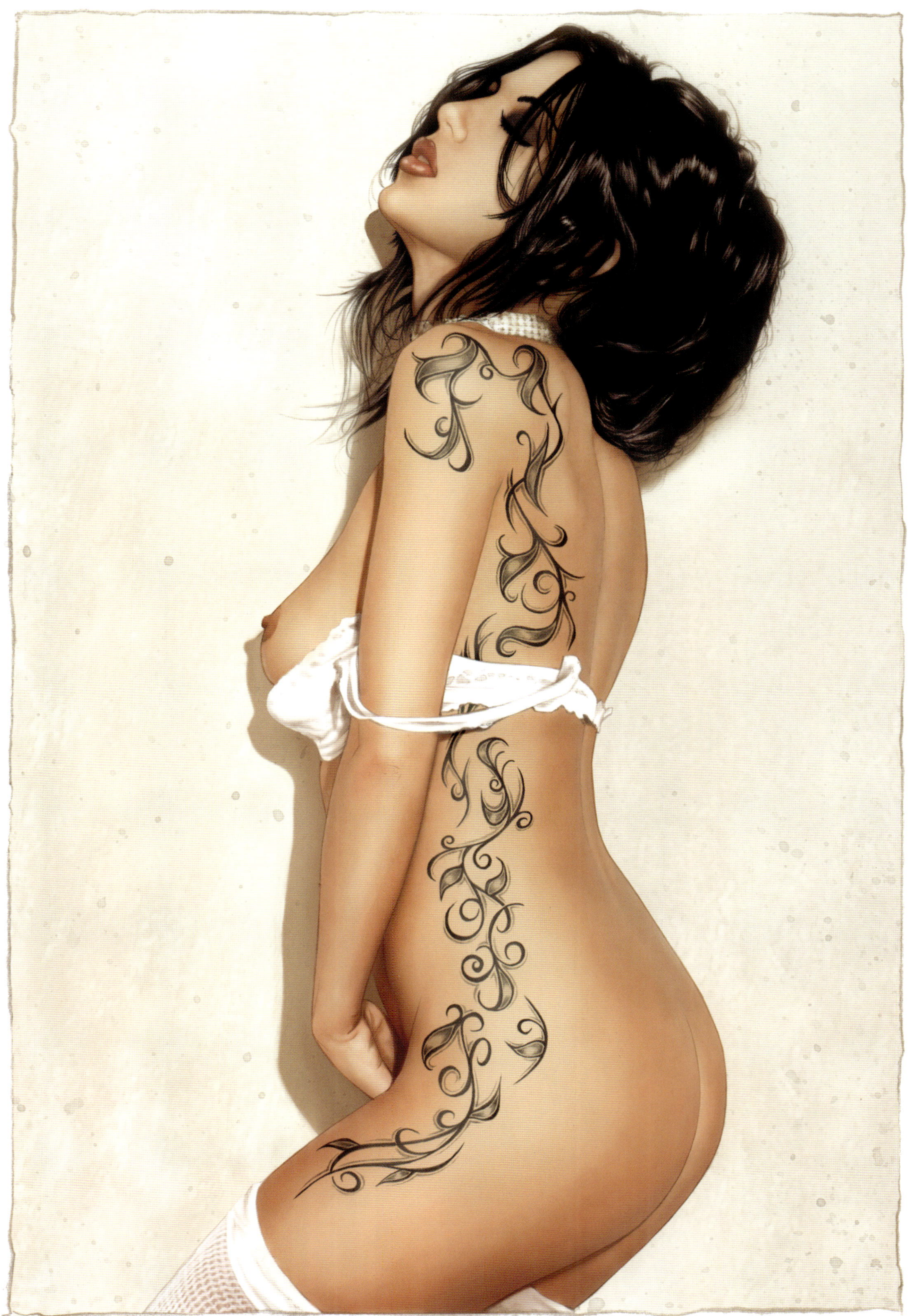

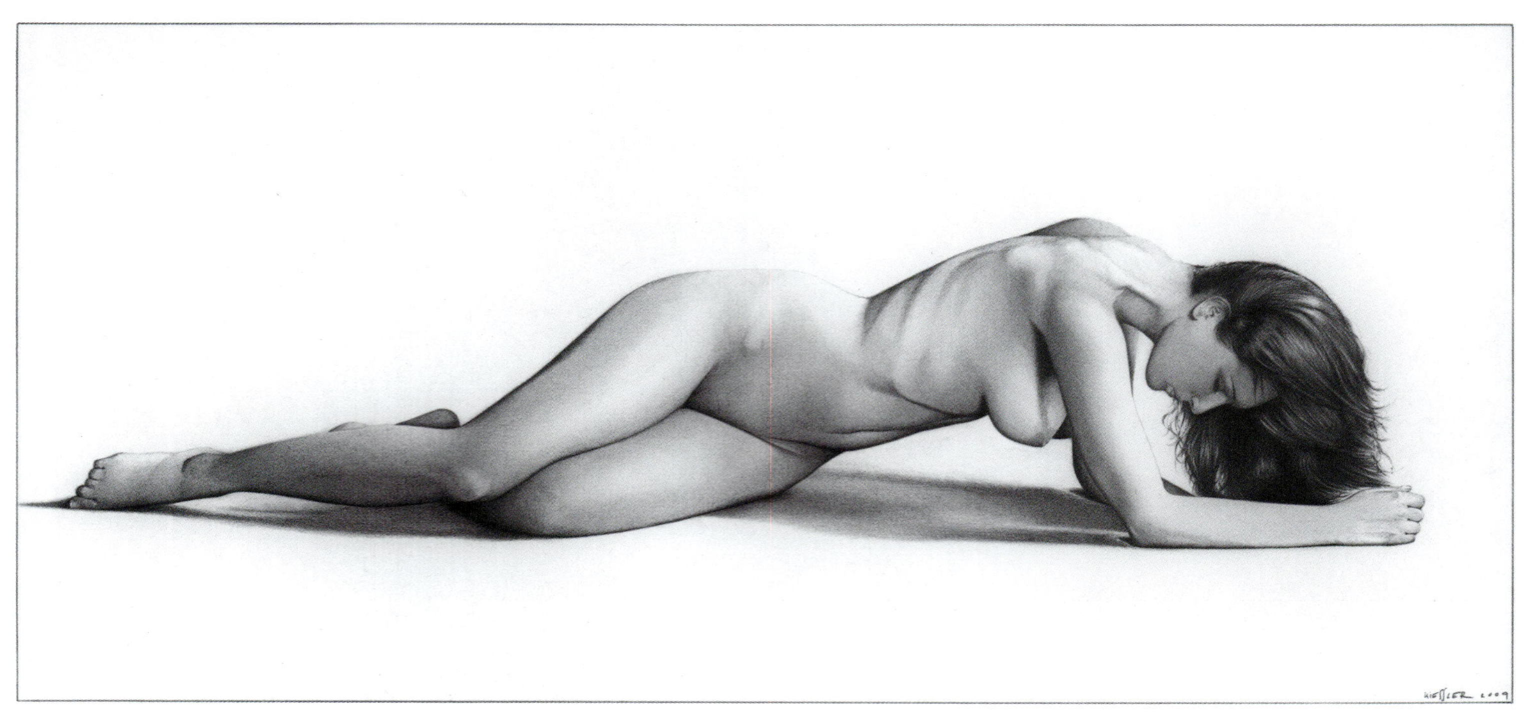

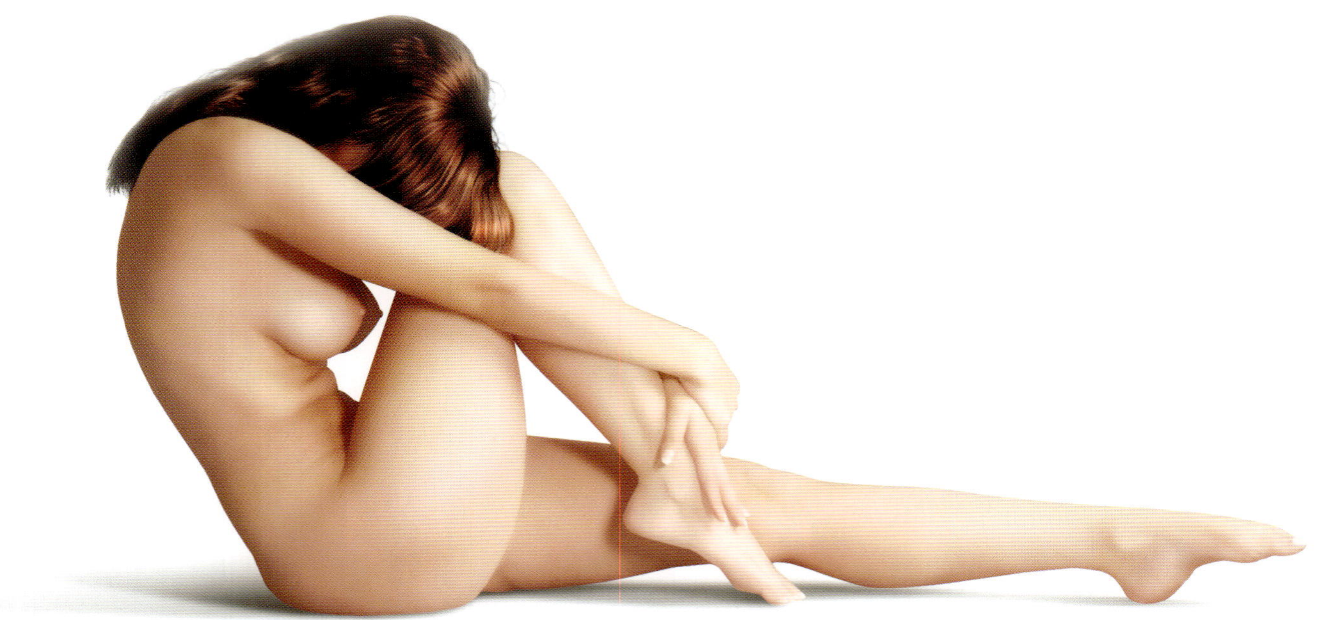

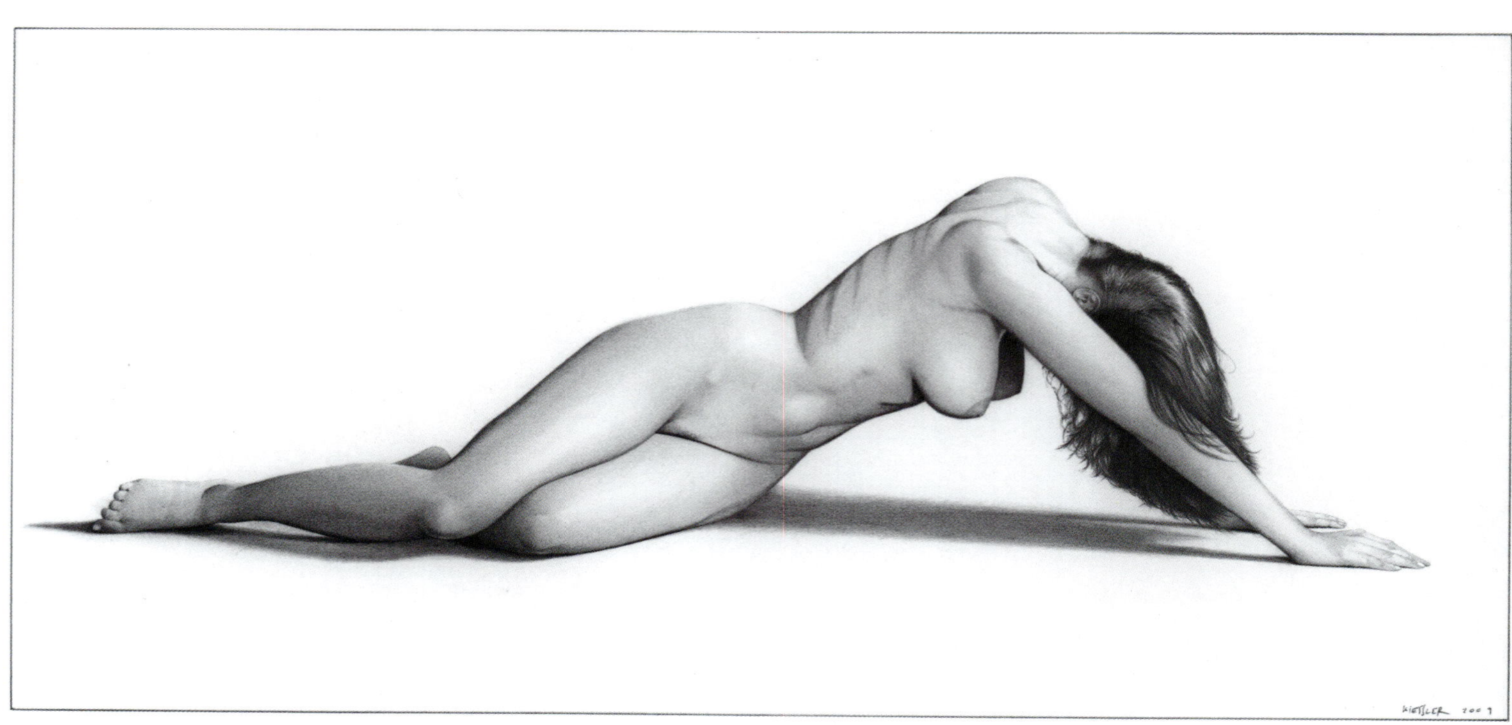

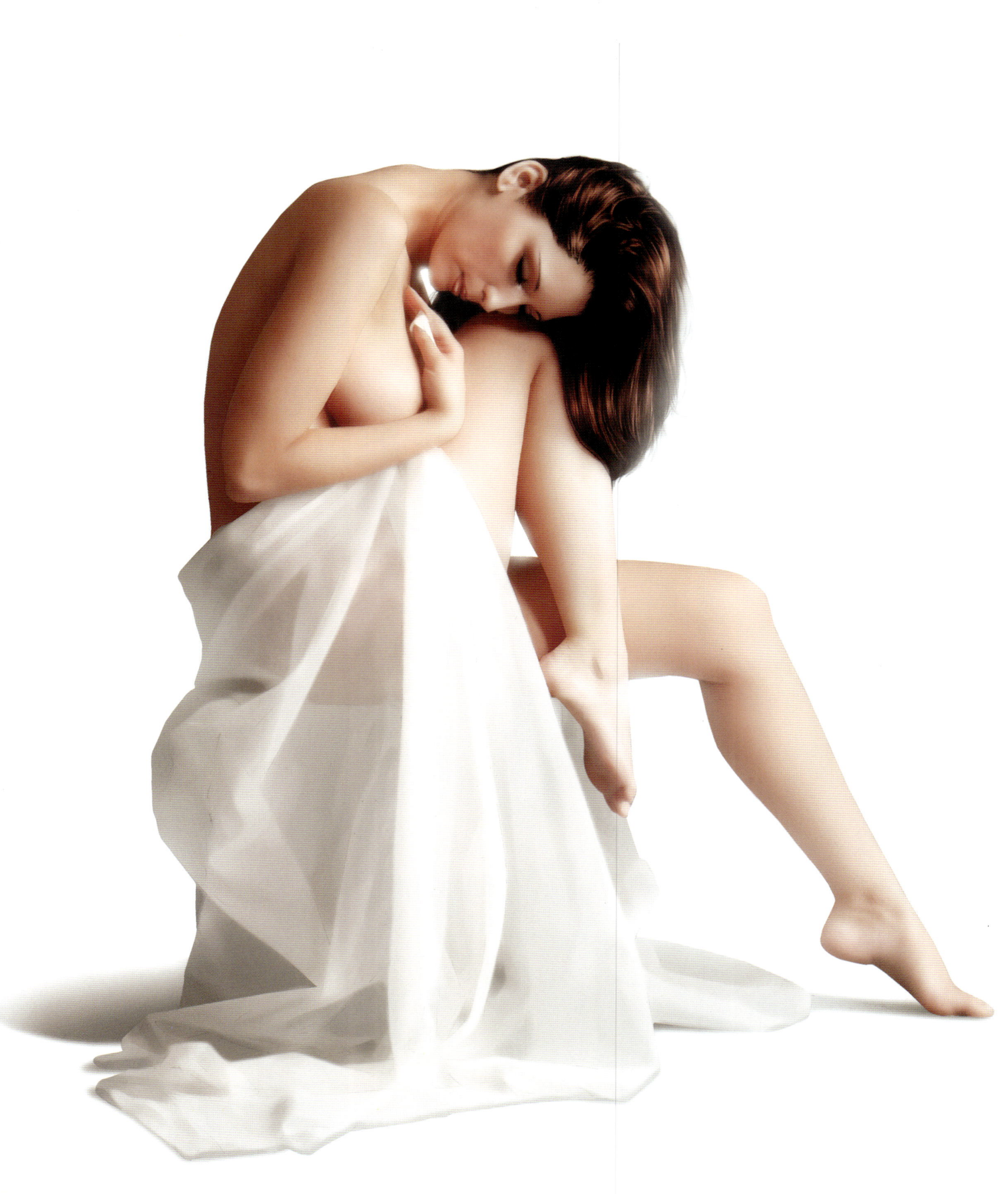

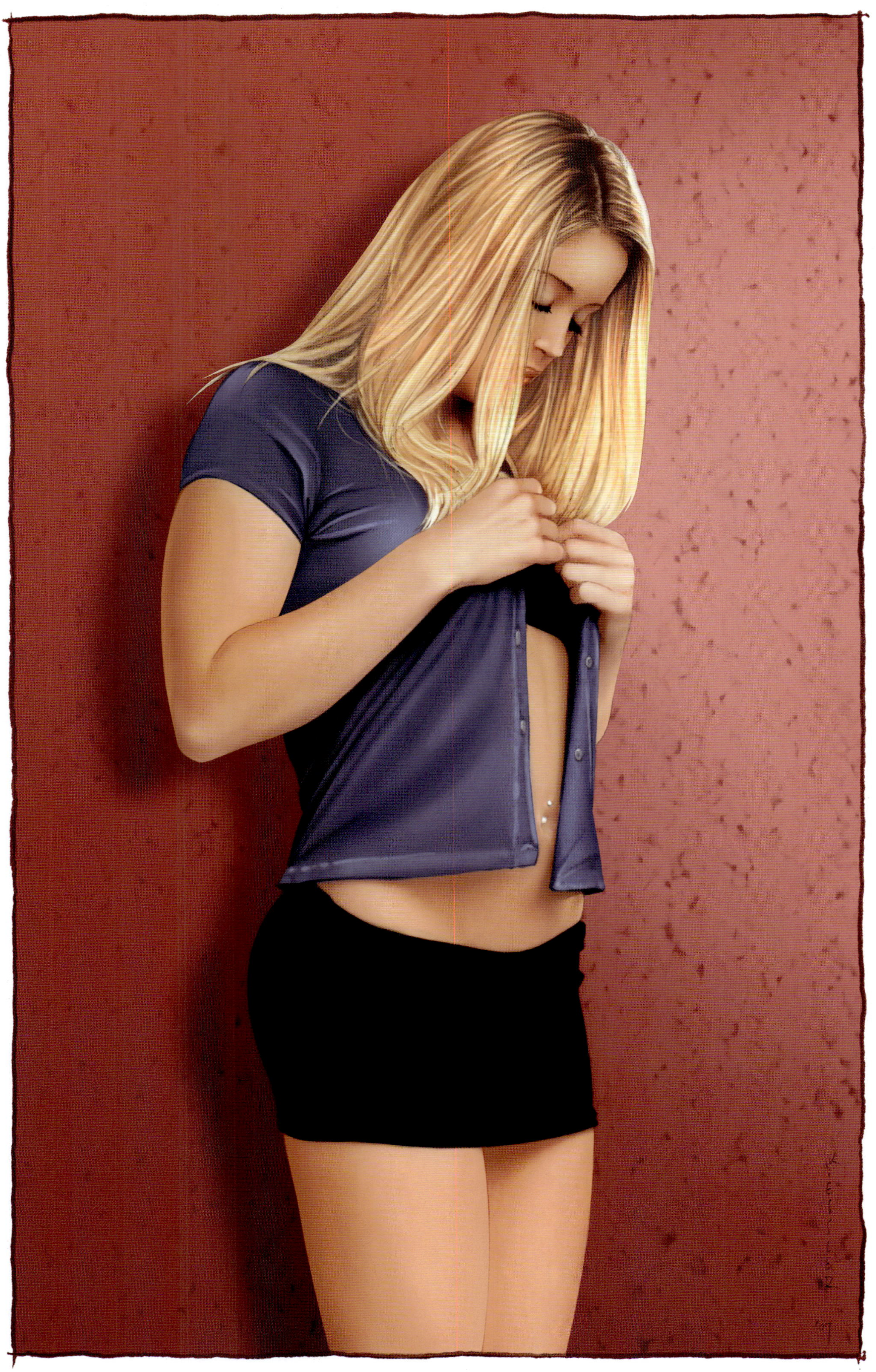

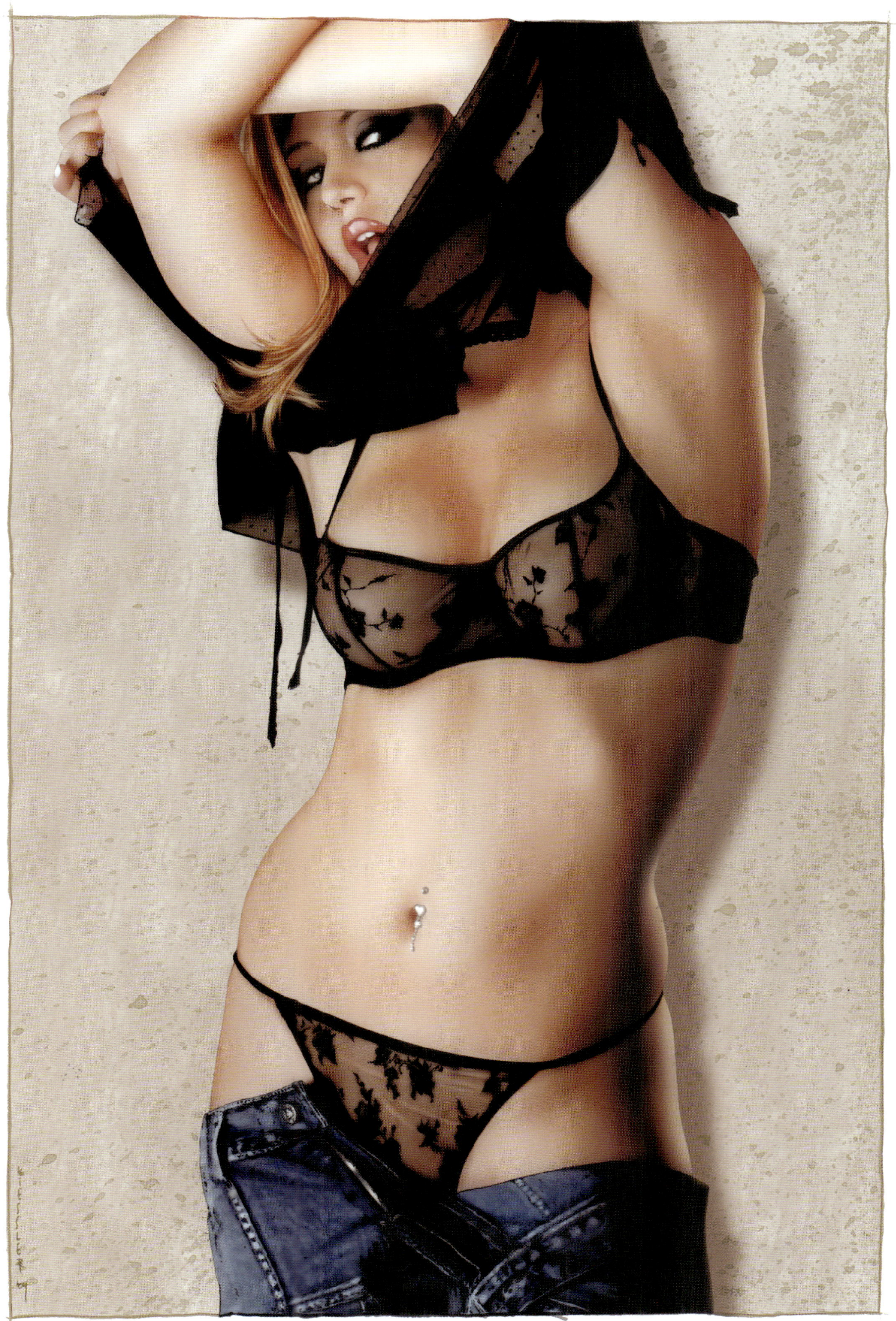

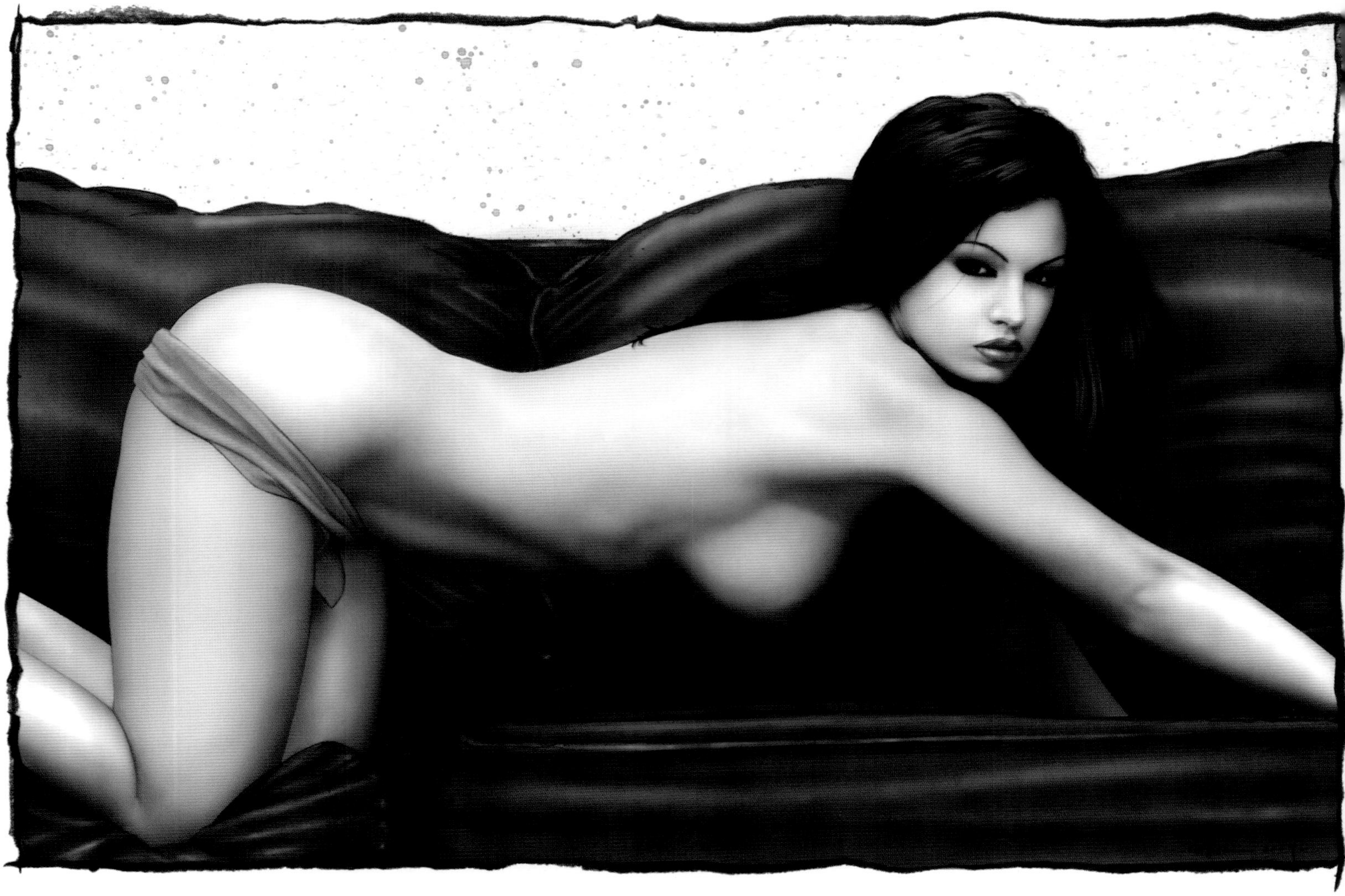

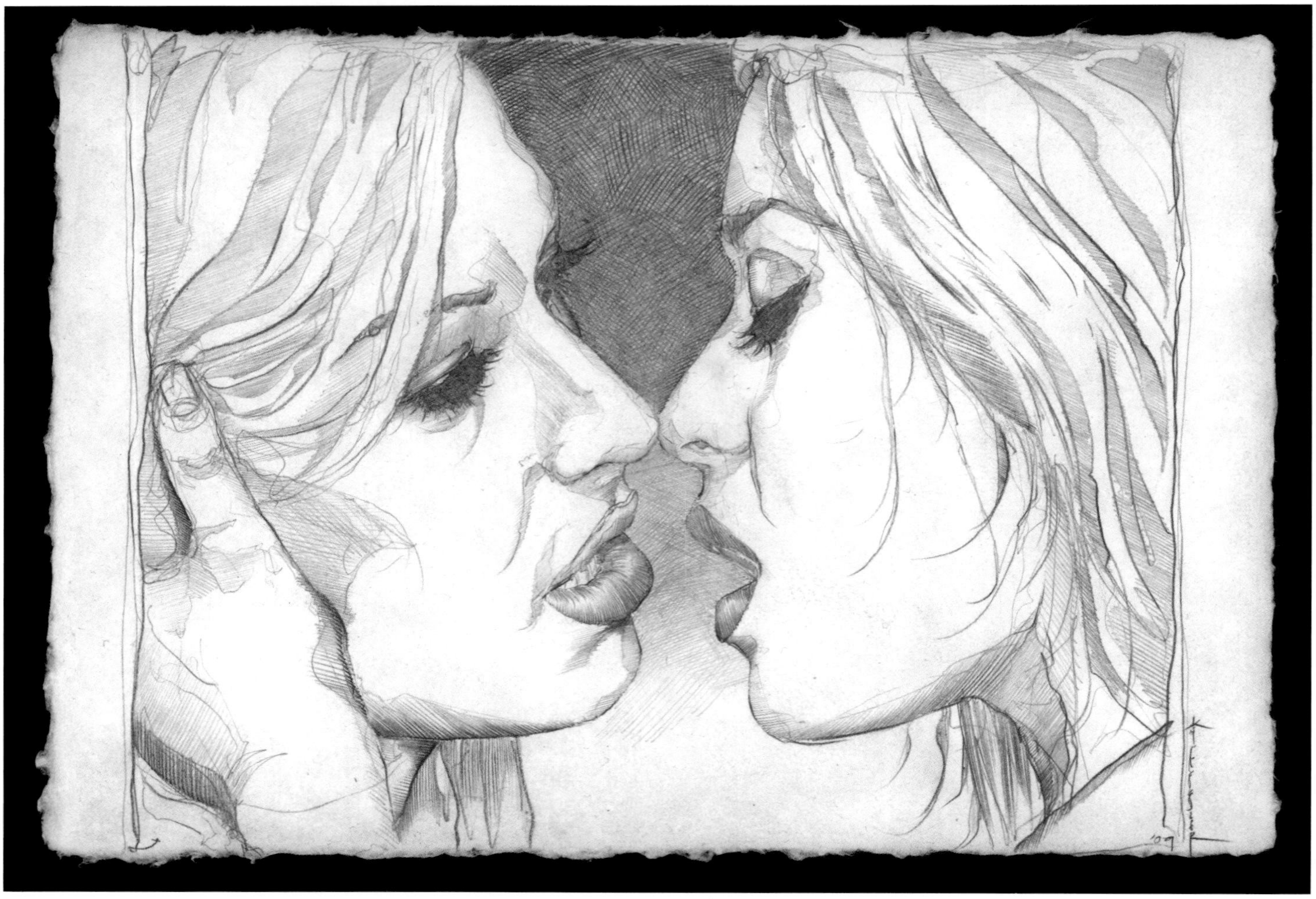

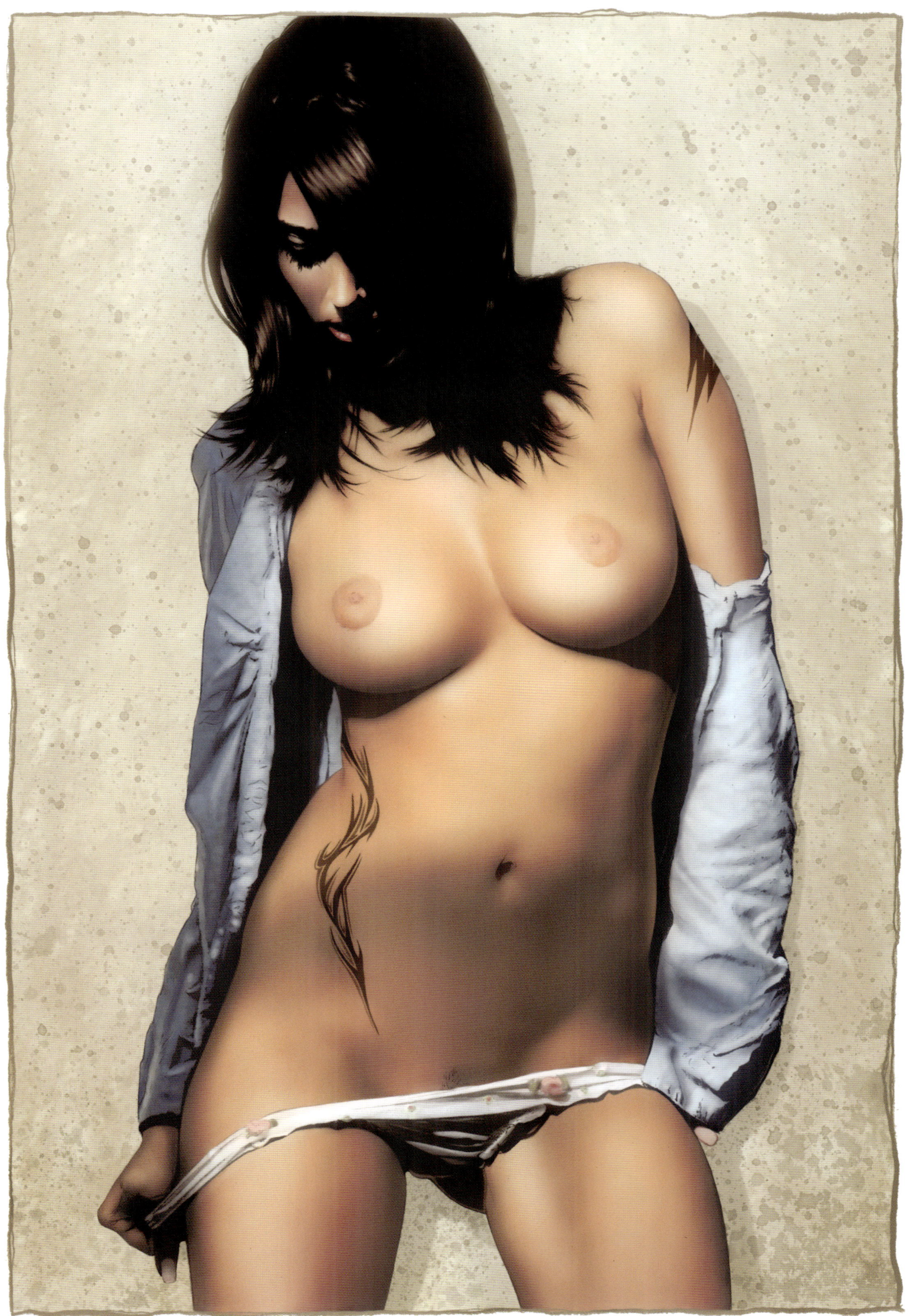

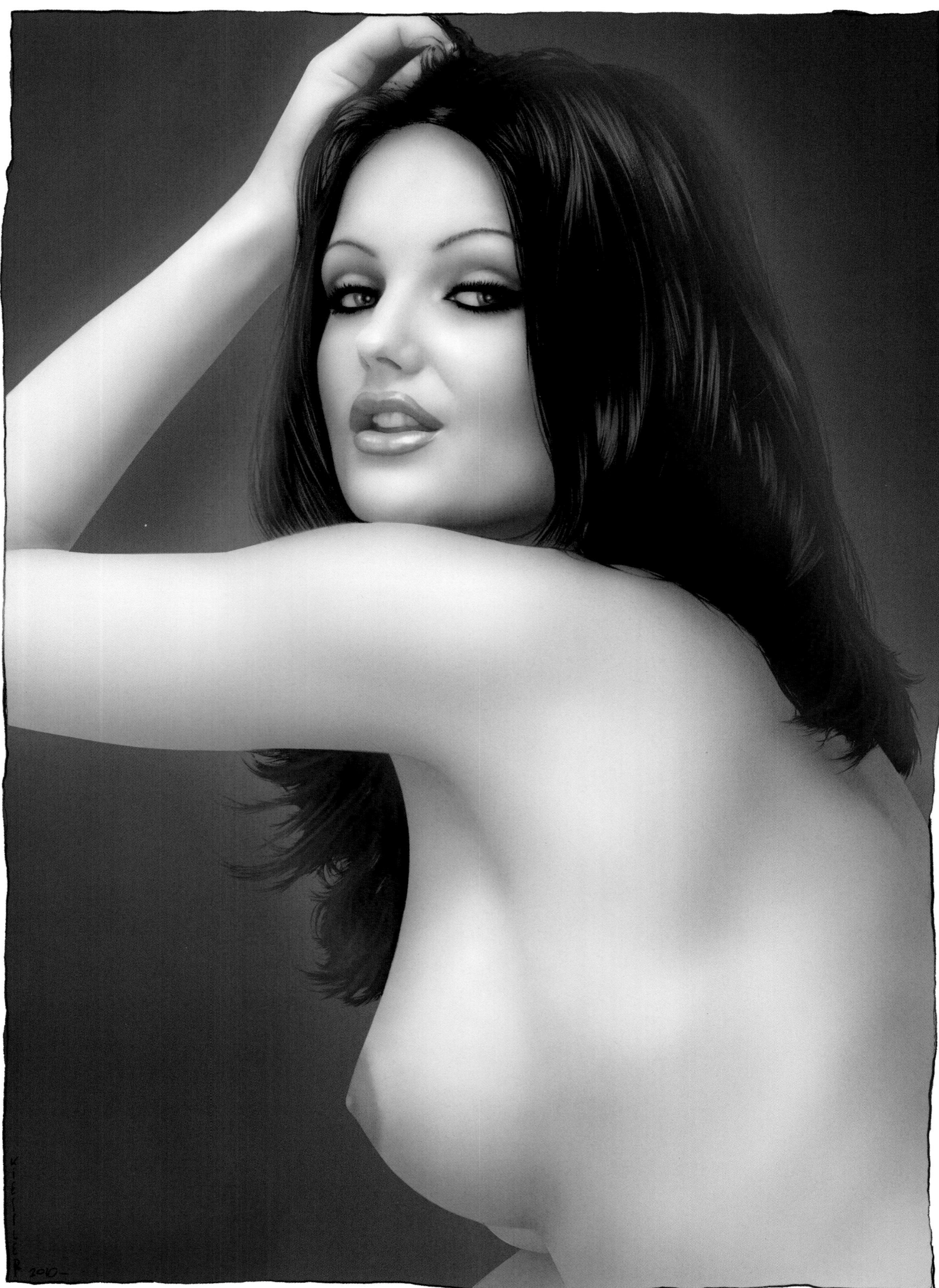

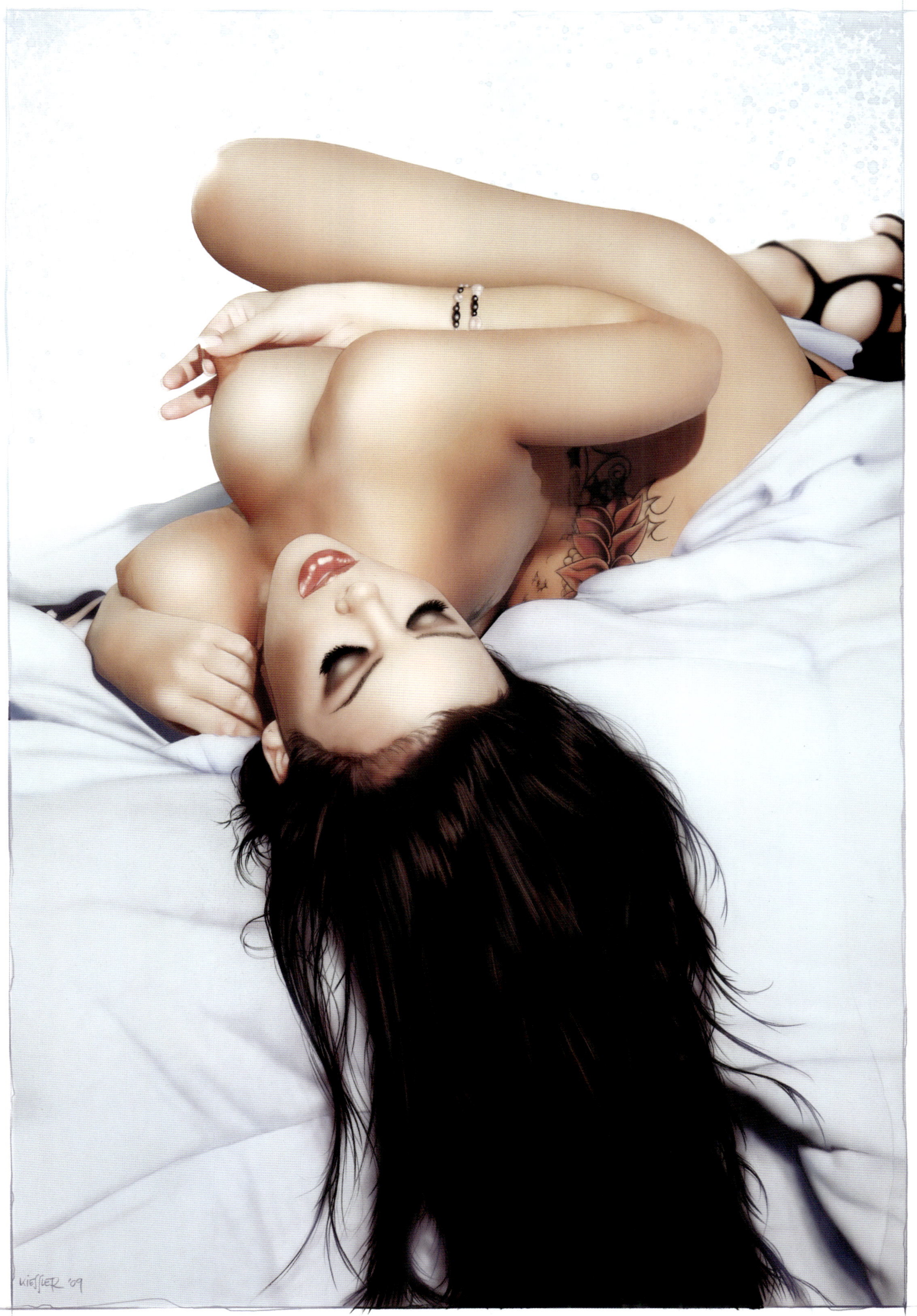
KIESSLER '09

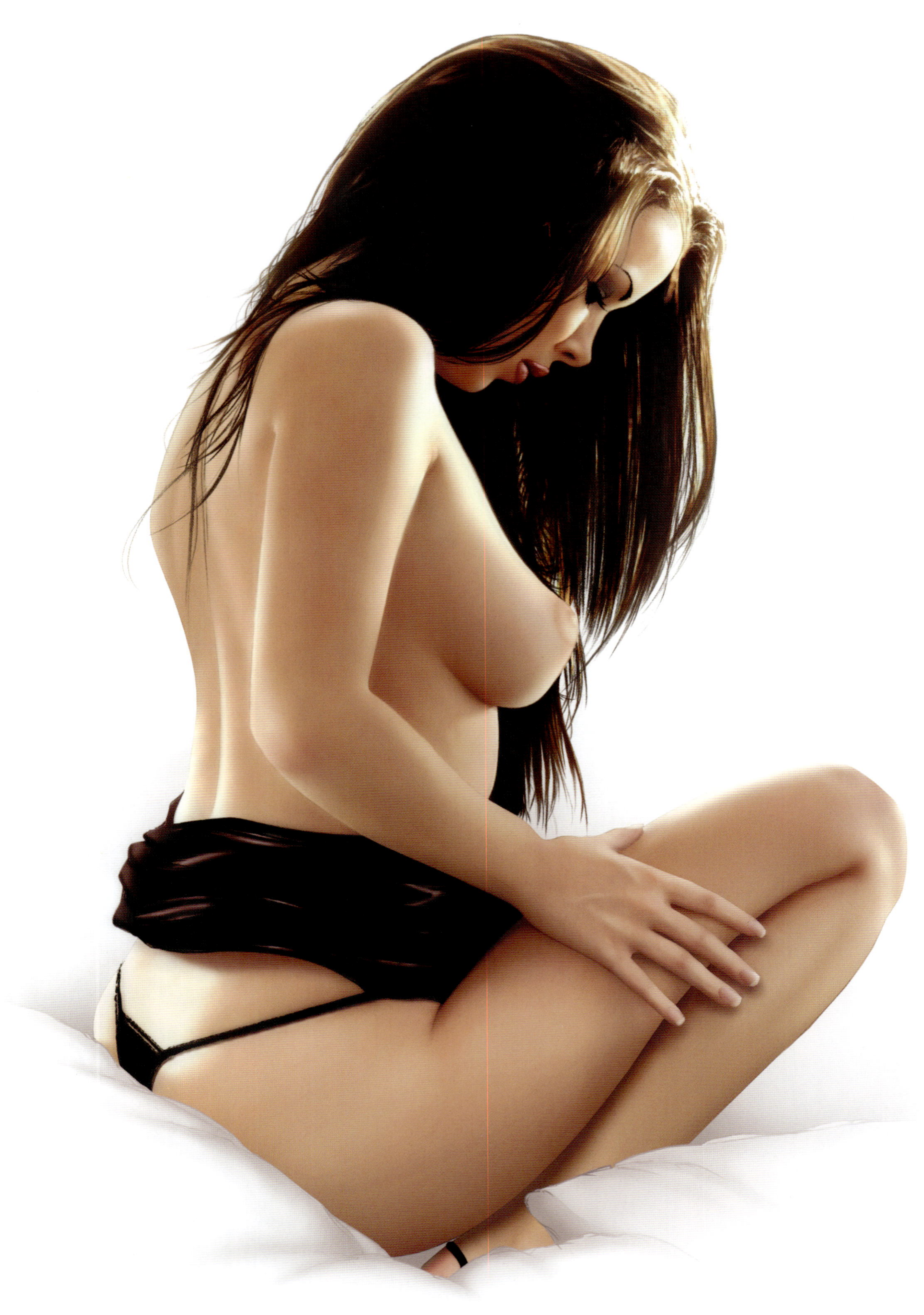

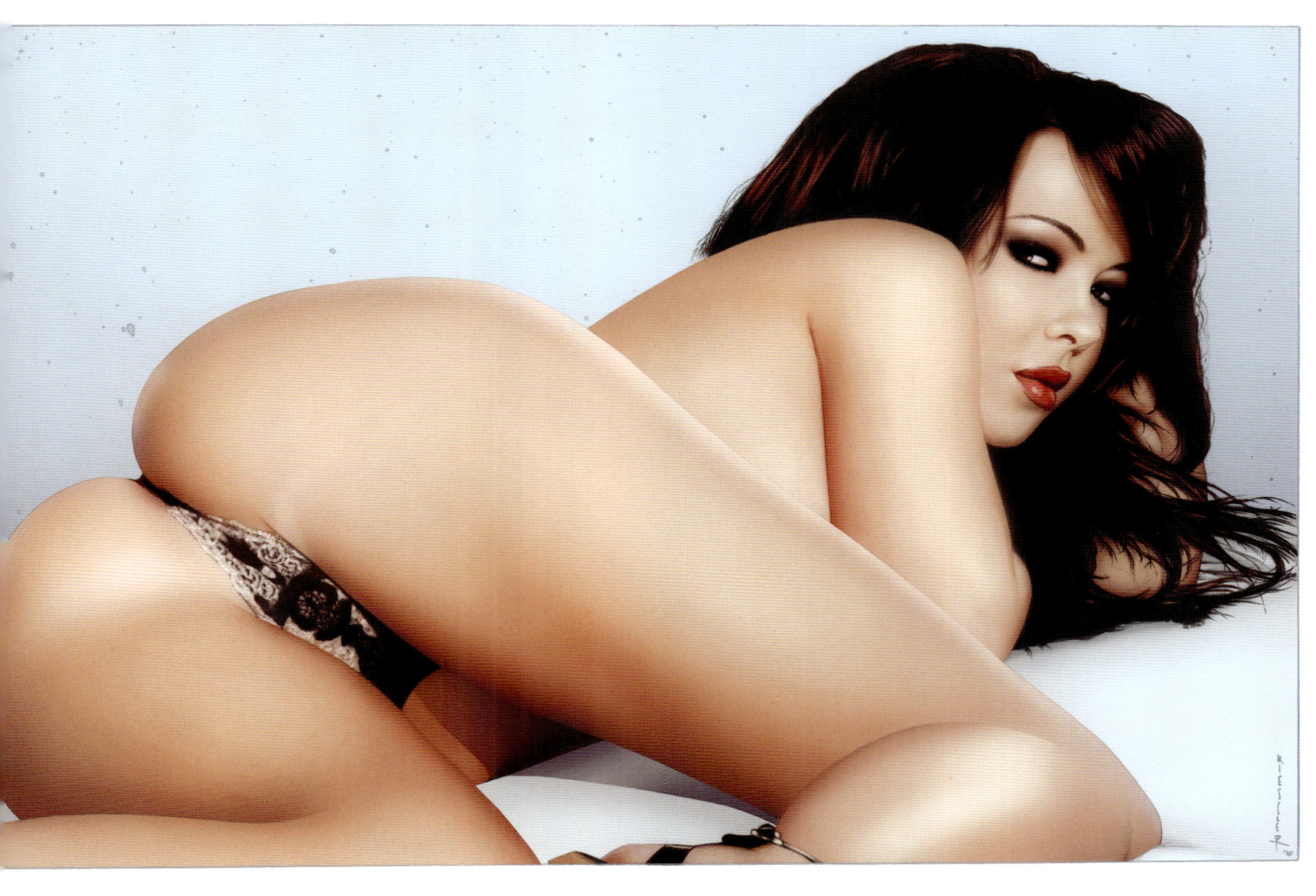

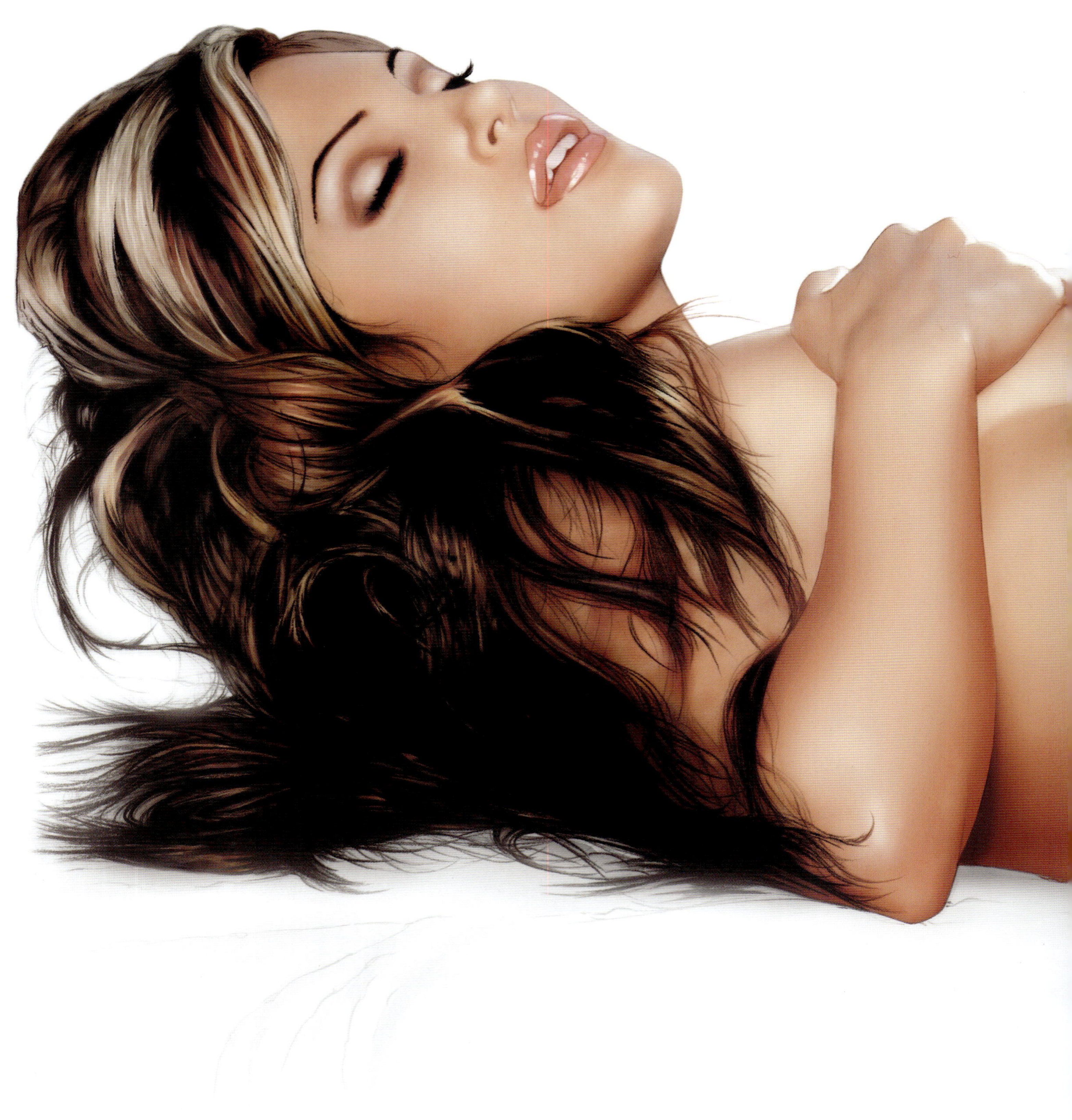

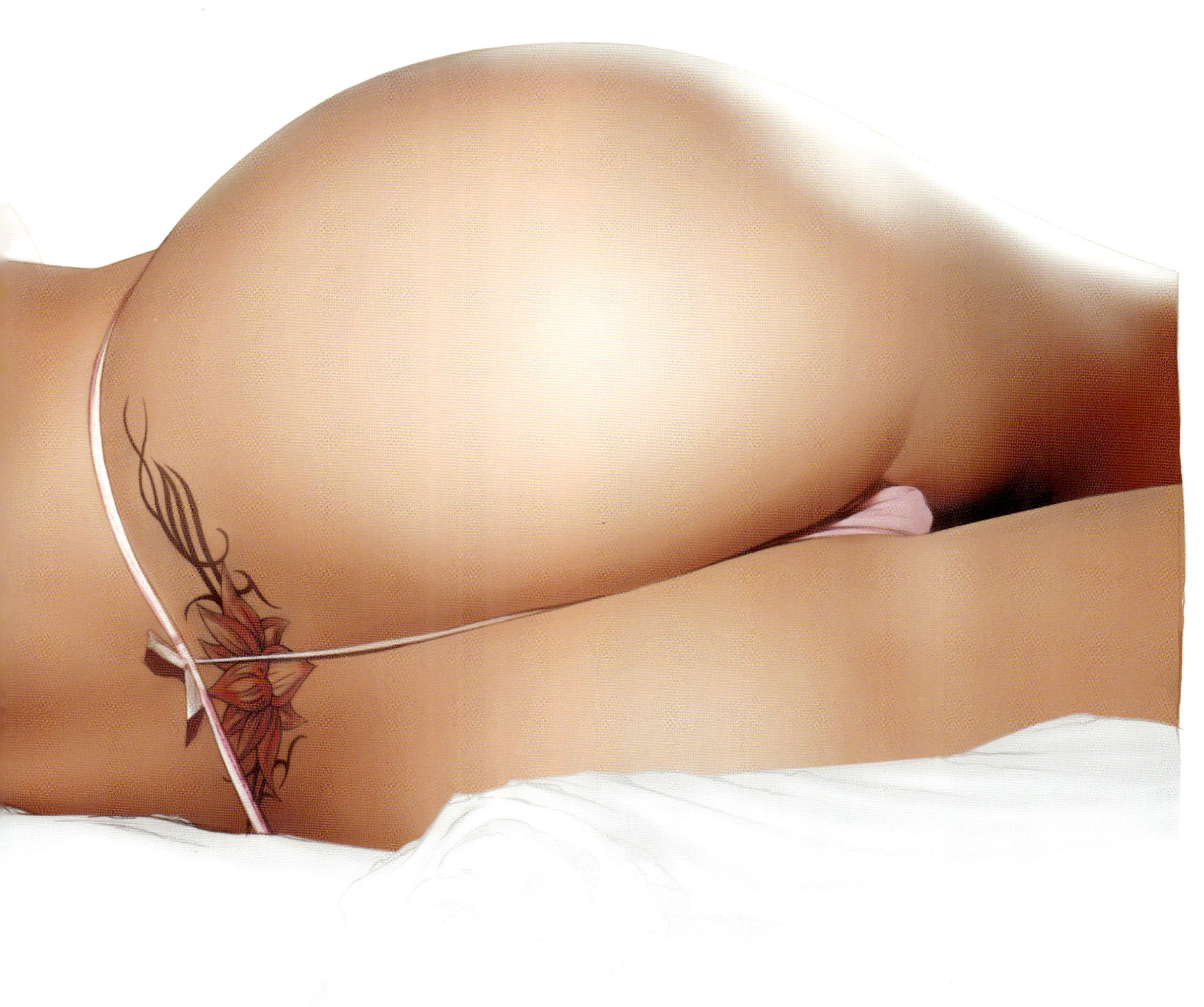

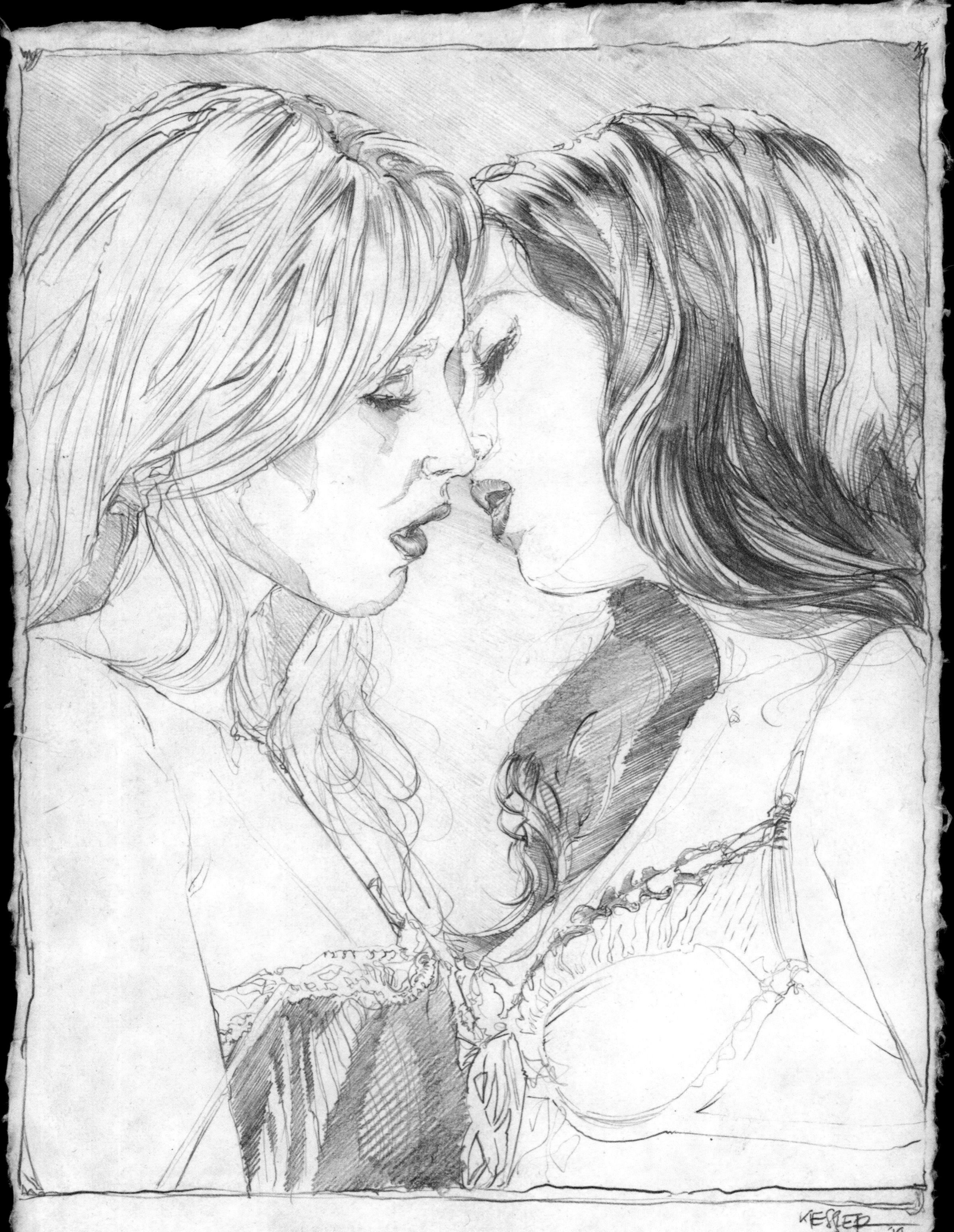
KESSLER '10

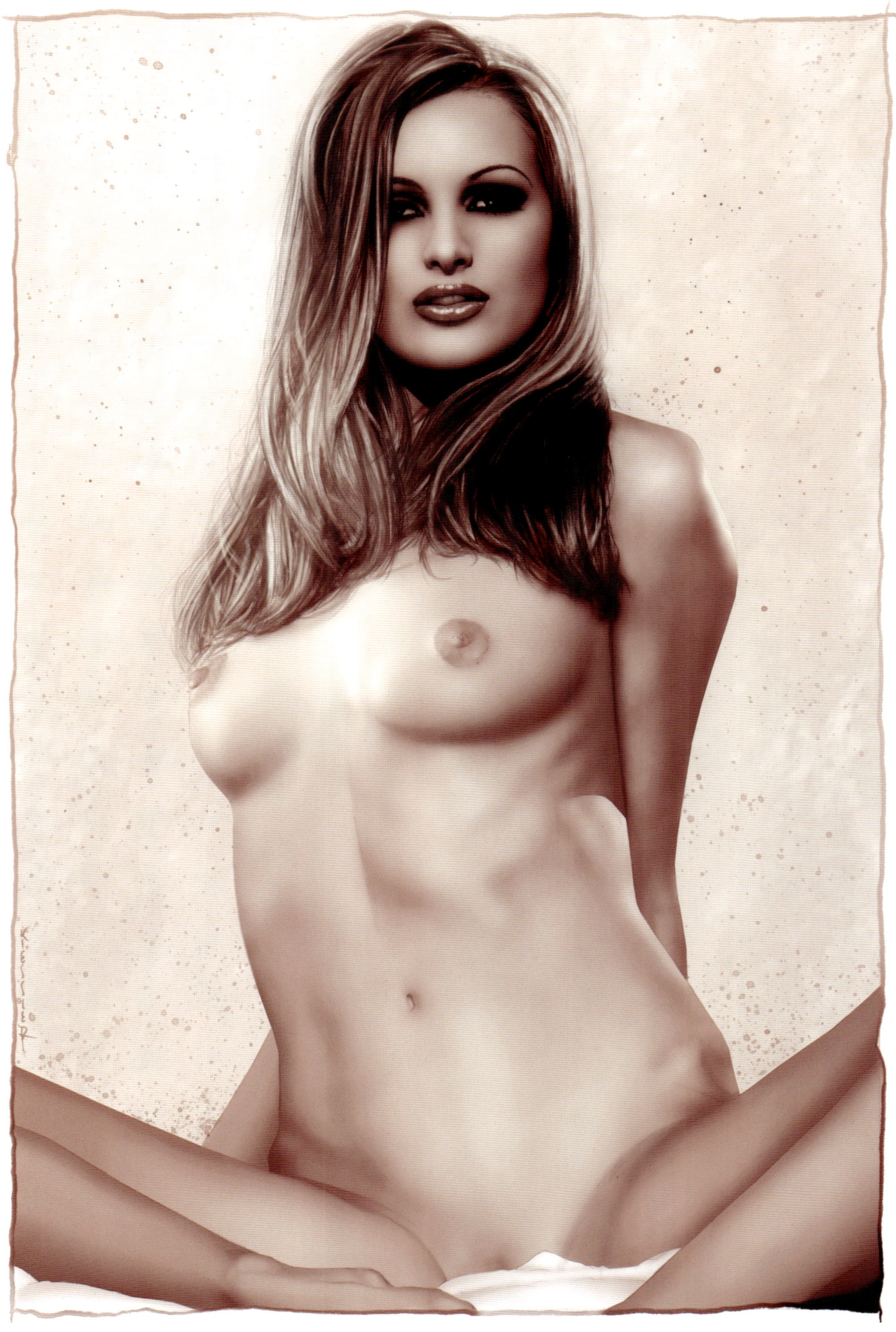

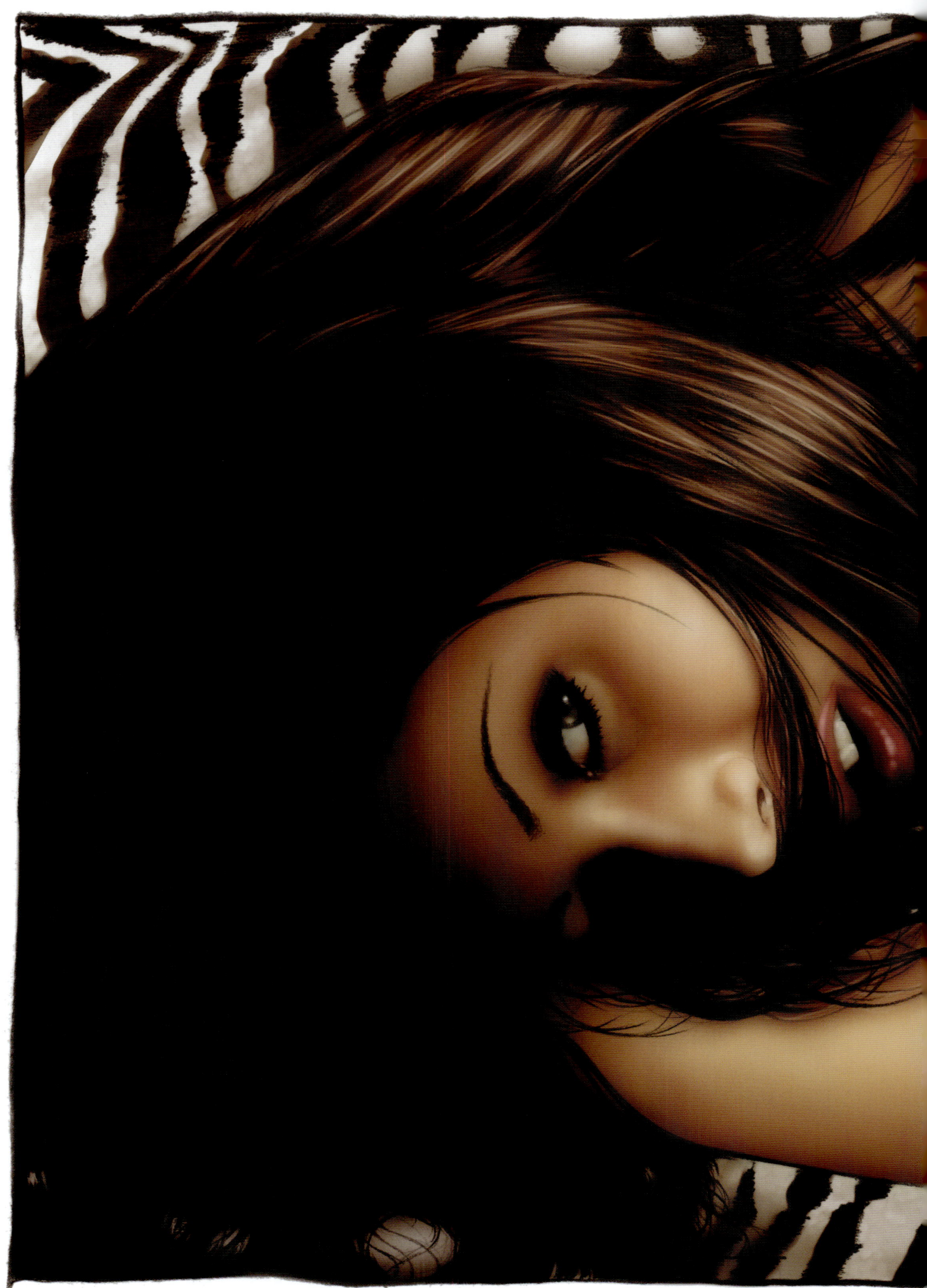

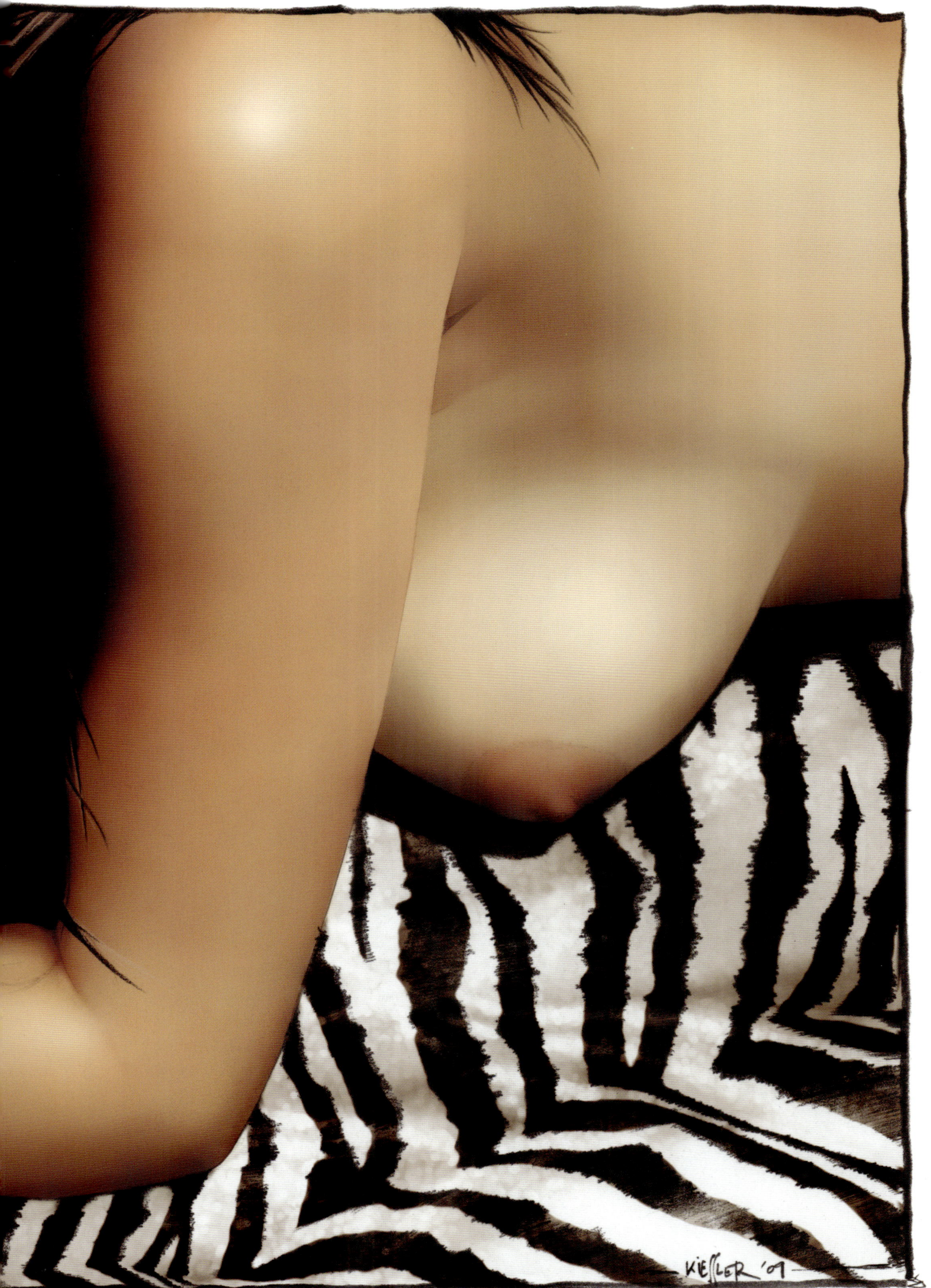
KIESSLER '07

Page 1	Natalia 2 v2. Photo by J. Stephen Hicks - www.hicksphoto.com
Page 2	Skull 1
Page 3	Natalia 8 v2. Photo by J. Stephen Hicks - www.hicksphoto.com
Page 4	Muse 1
Page 5	Shay. Photo by J. Stephen Hicks - www.hicksphoto.com
Page 6	Aisii 2. Photo by Daniel Ilinca - www.idaniphotography.com. Model: Aisii - www.aisii.daportfolio.com
Page 7	Aisii 1. Photo by Daniel Ilinca - www.idaniphotography.com. Model: Aisii - www.aisii.daportfolio.com
Page 8	Drakaina. Model: Drakaina - www.drakaina.com
Page 9	First Last Kiss. Photo by J. Stephen Hicks - www.hicksphoto.com
Page 10	Whatever 2 Sketch. Photo by J. Stephen Hicks - www.hicksphoto.com
Page 11	Whatever 2. Photo by J. Stephen Hicks - www.hicksphoto.com
Page 12-13	Whatever. Photo by J. Stephen Hicks - www.hicksphoto.com
Page 14	Nemesis. Model: Nemesis of www.suicidegirls.com
Page 15	Jana 2. Photo by J. Stephen Hicks - www.hicksphoto.com
Page 16	Sway 2. Model: Susan Wayland - www.susanwayland.de
Page 17	Pennelope. Model: Pennelope of www.suicidegirls.com
Page 18-19	Coming Out of the Dark. Photo by J. Stephen Hicks - www.hicksphoto.com
Page 20	Luscious 1 & 2. Model: Luscious of www.suicidegirls.com
Page 21	Luscious 3. Model: Luscious of www.suicidegirls.com
Page 22	Vintage. Photo by J. Stephen Hicks - www.hicksphoto.co
Page 23	Skull v2.
Page 24	Sway 1. Model: Susan Wayland - www.susanwayland.de
Page 25	Turquoise v2. Photo by www.marquis.de
Page 26	Pose 1 & 2. Photos by J. Stephen Hicks - www.hicksphoto.com
Page 27	Pose 3. Photo by J. Stephen Hicks - www.hicksphoto.com
Page 28-29	Martina. Photo by J. Stephen Hicks - www.hicksphoto.com
Page 30	Gone. Photo by J. Stephen Hicks - www.hicksphoto.com
Page 31	Touched 2. Photo by J. Stephen Hicks - www.hicksphoto.com
Page 32	Classic 1, 2, 3. Photo by Marcus Ranum - www.ranum.com. Model: Carly Champagne
Page 33	Classic 4. Photo by Marcus Ranum - www.ranum.com. Model: Carly Champagne
Page 34	Holly 3. Photo by J. Stephen Hicks - www.hicksphoto.com
Page 35	Holly 2. Photo by J. Stephen Hicks - www.hicksphoto.com
Page 36	Aria. Photo by J. Stephen Hicks - www.hicksphoto.com One Last Time. Photo by J. Stephen Hicks - www.hicksphoto.com
Page 37	The Blue Shirt. Photo by J. Stephen Hicks - www.hicksphoto.com
Page 38	Sandra. Photo by J. Stephen Hicks - www.hicksphoto.com
Page 39	Natalia 6. Photo by J. Stephen Hicks - www.hicksphoto.com
Page 40	Natalia 7. Photo by J. Stephen Hicks - www.hicksphoto.com
Page 41	Natalia 9. Photo by J. Stephen Hicks - www.hicksphoto.com
Page 42-43	Temptation. Photo by J. Stephen Hicks - www.hicksphoto.com
Page 44	The Girls. Photo by J. Stephen Hicks - www.hicksphoto.com
Page 45	Icon. Photo by J. Stephen Hicks - www.hicksphoto.com
Page 46-47	Down. Photo by J. Stephen Hicks - www.hicksphoto.com

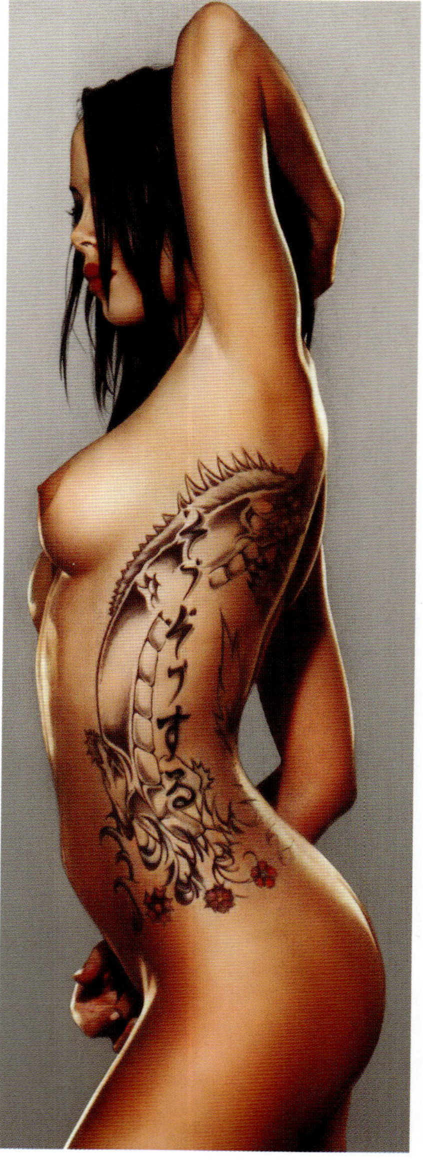

Image selection, graphite, pencils and inks by Daniel Kiessler (danielkiessler.com)

Digital coloring by José Augusto Cano Martinez (http://canoart.net)

Thank you to all the photographers and models I had the pleasure to work with on this book.